# Brilliancies and Blunders
## in the
## European Bridge Championship

**MAXWELL MACMILLAN BRIDGE SERIES**

*Publishing Editor:* Glyn Liggins

*In preparation:*
FLINT, J. & NORTH, F.
Tiger Bridge Revisited

REESE, T. & BIRD, D.
Famous Hands from Famous Matches

SENIOR, B.
Bread and Butter Bidding

SMITH, N.
Bridge Literature

CROWHURST, E.
Acol — The Complete System

HACKETT, P.
Bridge Around the World

A full catalogue of Maxwell Macmillan Bridge books is available from:
**Maxwell Macmillan Bridge**
**London Road, Wheatley, Oxford OX9 1YR**

# Brilliancies and Blunders
## in the
# European Bridge Championship

## Terence Reese

The 1991 European Championship was
played at the Great Southern Hotel,
Killarney, from Sunday June 16th
to Saturday June 29th.

**MAXWELL MACMILLAN BRIDGE**

## MAXWELL MACMILLAN INTERNATIONAL PUBLISHING GROUP

| | |
|---|---|
| EUROPE/<br>MIDDLE EAST/AFRICA | Maxwell Macmillan International,<br>Hollow Way, Cowley, Oxford OX4 2YH, England<br>Tel: (0865) 748754   Fax: (0865) 748808 |
| U.S.A. | Macmillan Publishing Company<br>866 Third Avenue, New York, NY 10022<br>Tel: (212) 702-2000   Fax: (212) 605-9341 |
| CANADA | 1200 Eglinton Avenue East,<br>Suite 200, Don Mills, Ontario M3C 3N1, Canada<br>Tel: (416) 449-6030   Fax: (416) 449-0068 |
| AUSTRALIA/<br>NEW ZEALAND | Lakes Business Park, Building A1,<br>2 Lord Street, Botany, NSW 20119, Australia<br>Tel: (02) 316-9444   Fax: (02) 316-9485 |
| ASIA/PACIFIC<br>(Except Japan) | 72 Hillview Avenue,<br>103-00 Tacam House, Singapore 2366<br>Tel: (65) 769-6000   Fax: (65) 769-3731 |
| LATIN AMERICA | 28100 US Highway 19 North,<br>Suite 200, Clearwater, FL 34621<br>Tel: (813) 725-4033   Fax: (813) 725-2185 |
| JAPAN | 8th Floor, Matsuoka Central Building,<br>1-7-1 Nishishinjuku, Shinjuku-Ku, Tokyo 160, Japan<br>Tel: 81-3-3344-5201   Fax: 81-3-3344-5202 |

---

First edition 1991

**Library of Congress Cataloging in Publication Data Applied for**

**Cataloguing in Publication Data can be obtained from the British Library**

ISBN 1 85744 500 7

Cover design by Jeanne Lambert
Typeset by Lands Services, East Molesey and
Printed in Great Britain by BPCC Wheatons Ltd, Exeter

# Foreword

This book was written from day to day as the tournament
progressed. Not a word was altered or added in the light
of subsequent events. If my prognostications look foolish
at the end, I shall have to bear it.

Terence Reese

# Contents

Our thanks to Mark Huba
who provided the photographs for this book.

# The Line-up

A golfing and tourist centre, Killarney has a large number of hotels and guest houses, making it a fine venue for the three sections of the European Championship. The Open Teams, Ladies Teams and Ladies Pairs will all be played at the Conference Centre of the Great Southern Hotel.

# The Open Teams

Despite two late withdrawals there will be 26 teams in the Open, easily a record. Some of the countries are not precisely in Europe but are members of the European Bridge League.

Each country will play a match of 32 boards against each other country, starting on Sunday June 16th and finishing on Sunday 23rd.

The holders, Poland, must be reckoned the favourites, about 3 to 1 on the bookmakers' lists. The biggest danger may be the French, about 5 to 1. They are missing some of their best known stars (no Chemla, Mari or Perron), but Quantin and Abécassis, in particular, have been in great form lately.

Polish players perform with distinction in all the big European events. One must say that it is difficult to distinguish between them, so I won't try. (At the prize-giving after an event in London David Burn remarked wittily that all their names would win big scores at Scrabble.)

In the next group of teams sure to do well are Sweden, Austria and Italy, all recent winners. Israel is usually thereabouts. Players from Norway, the Netherlands, and Greece have been in fine form recently.

The British team is Forrester–Robson, Armstrong–Kirby, Sowter–Smolski. Robson is a young (6′ 6″) player who has done exceptionally well with Forrester in international pairs events. The others are all veterans of the championship. If I were foolish enough to make a forecast, I would say that between third and fifth might be their mark.

Every team has a non-playing captain, who names the team to begin each match and may change the line-up at half time. Some countries also have a 'coach', whose main function at this stage is to study the methods of opposing teams and suggest counter-measures. The British captain is Sandra Landy, the coach David Burn.

# The Ladies Teams

There are 17 entries, again each country playing a match of 32 boards against each other country. Form in the Ladies event is more variable than in the Open, but it is reasonable to expect Sweden, Denmark, France, Netherlands, and Italy to be thereabouts at the finish.

The British team is Nicola Smith (formerly Gardener) and Pat Davies, Elizabeth McGowan and Sandra Penfold, Vi Mitchell and Jane Preddy, with Chris Dixon as n.p.c. Smith and Davies are a front-rank pair, the others have something to prove.

The Ladies, with a shorter programme, will take the field on Wednesday June 19th.

# Ladies Pairs Championship

The Ladies Pairs Championship begins with three qualifying rounds, with a carry-over to a two-session final. There are 13 British pairs in the field, but France has the strongest guns.

# How matches are scored

In the team events each deal is scored separately, with a comparison based on International Match Points, whose effect is to reduce the difference between big swings and small ones. At the end of the match the IMPs are converted into Victory Points. There is normally a division of 30VPs between the two teams, but the maximum for the winners is 25; the losers in this case score from 0 to 5 according to the measure of their defeat. The final result depends on the total of VPs, any tie being broken according to the match between the tying teams.

The principal sponsor of the championship is the
GENERALI INSURANCE GROUP.

# Day One

## Norway v. Ireland

It is usual for the home side to play the first match on Bridgerama and this one, as it happens, looked the most interesting of the round. The Irish team (among bridge players there is no nonsense about North and South) contains two very experienced pairs, while the Norwegians have some fine young players who are expected to represent Europe in the next World Youth Championship.

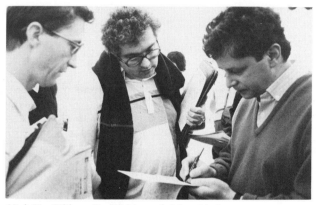

*Nick FitzGibbon, Pat Walshe and Adam Mesbur compare scores.*

Some dull boards at first, but then:

*Love all; Dealer West.*

|  | ♠ K Q 2 |  |
|---|---|---|
|  | ♡ 10 8 7 5 4 |  |
|  | ◇ Q J 4 |  |
|  | ♣ 8 6 |  |

| ♠ 8 | | ♠ A 10 9 5 3 |
|---|---|---|
| ♡ Q 9 6 | N W E S | ♡ None |
| ◇ K 10 8 7 5 3 | | ◇ A 9 6 |
| ♣ A 9 2 | | ♣ K J 10 5 3 |

|  | ♠ J 7 6 4 |  |
|---|---|---|
|  | ♡ A K J 3 2 |  |
|  | ◇ 2 |  |
|  | ♣ Q 7 4 |  |

To put you in the mood, what do you suppose was the opening bid by the Irish West?

**Closed room**

| West | North | East | South |
|------|-------|------|-------|
| *Boland* | *Hoeyland* | *Walshe* | *Hoeyland* |
| 2♠ | Pass | 4◇ | All Pass |

North-South were a fraternal combination. West's two spades denoted a weak two in one of the minors. Such is life. East recorded 12 tricks, 170 to Ireland.

**Open room**

| West | North | East | South |
|------|-------|------|-------|
| *Groetheim* | *Mesbur* | *Helgemo* | *Fitzgibbon* |
| Pass | Pass | 1♠ | 2♡ |
| 3◇ | 4♡ | Pass | Pass |
| Double | All Pass | | |

South's intervention on borderline values which included good defence against spades was certainly unwise. The defence was brilliant. West led a spade to the ace, ruffed the return, played a diamond to the ace and ruffed another spade. Then came ace and another club, followed by a fourth spade, on which West made his third trump trick. It was four down (800 these days) and a swing of 11 match points to Norway.

# Norway v. Ireland (second half)

The Irish were 12 points down at half-time and began the second half disastrously, losing points on almost all the early boards. They began a recovery on this deal:

*Game all; Dealer East.*

```
                    ♠ K J 5 2
                    ♡ J 8
                    ◇ A J 9 3
                    ♣ 7 3 2
    ♠ 10 8                            ♠ 9 7 3
    ♡ A Q 10 9 7 5 3    ┌─────────┐   ♡ K 6 4 2
    ◇ 6 4 2            │   N     │   ◇ 5
    ♣ J               │ W   E   │   ♣ K 10 9 8 4
                      │   S     │
                      └─────────┘
                    ♠ A Q 6 4
                    ♡ None
                    ◇ K Q 10 8 7
                    ♣ A Q 6 5
```

**Closed room**

| West | North | East | South |
|------|-------|------|-------|
| *Boland* | *Thomassen* | *Walshe* | *Hantveit* |
| | | Pass | 1♣ |
| 3♡ | 3♠ | 5♡ | 6♡ |
| Pass | 6♠ | All Pass | |

Six spades looks easy. In a sense there are 13 tricks, if you include two heart ruffs and the club finesse. However, East led a tricky four of clubs and the declarer went up with dummy's ace. He drew two rounds of trumps, crossed to hand with a diamond and ruffed the second heart. Now he needed the second round of diamonds to stand up — but it didn't.

This looks pretty inept on the declarer's part, but it turned out that on his side of the screen he had been told (correctly) by East that West's three hearts denoted a heart-club two-suiter. Apparently there is no redress when an opponent (West) has forgotten the system; quite wrong.

## Open room

| West | North | East | South |
|------|-------|------|-------|
| *Hoeyland* | *Brennan* | *Hoeyland* | *Scannell* |
| | | Pass | 1 ♢ |
| 2 ♡ | Double | 4 ♡ | 4 ♠ |
| 5 ♡ | Double | Pass | 6 ♣ |
| Pass | 6 ♠ | All Pass | |

This time the jack of clubs was led from the West side and the play was easy. It was a swing of 17 points. Most of the remaining boards were bad for Ireland and the margin was 25–5. The young Norwegians look very strong.

*Frenetic activity in the scoring tent after the end of play.*

# Britain v. Turkey

Sometimes there are only eight tricks in view, but the ninth will appear in a way difficult to foresee.

*North-South game; Dealer East.*

```
                    ♠ A 4 3
                    ♡ 9 7 6 5 4
                    ◇ 8 6 4
                    ♣ A 10
  ♠ 7 6 2          ┌─────────┐        ♠ K Q 5
  ♡ A J 10 8       │    N    │        ♡ K Q 2
  ◇ Q 9            │ W     E │        ◇ J 7 3 2
  ♣ K Q 5 2        │    S    │        ♣ J 7 4
                    └─────────┘
                    ♠ J 10 9 8
                    ♡ 3
                    ◇ A K 10 5
                    ♣ 9 8 6 3
```

**Closed room**

| West | North | East | South |
|------|-------|------|-------|
| Armstrong | Ozdil | Kirby | Kubac |
|  |  | Pass | Pass |
| 1 NT | Pass | 2 ♠ | Pass |
| 2 NT | All Pass |  |  |

East's two spades was equal to a raise to 2NT. West did not fancy the chances of game opposite a passed hand, and he duly registered 120.

**Open room**

| West | North | East | South |
|------|-------|------|-------|
| Assael | Forrester | Zorlu | Robson |
|  |  | 1 ♣ | Pass |
| 1 ♡ | Pass | 1 NT | Pass |
| 3 NT | All Pass |  |  |

This time East had opened, so West was not going to stay short of game.

South led the jack of spades to the ace and a spade was returned. East played a club to the queen and ace and the spades were cleared. At this point East had eight tricks in view, but no more unless the clubs were breaking 3–3. Looking at it in another way, the defenders had made two tricks and three more were in sight — all in the South hand.

Four rounds of hearts proved awkward for South. From the fact that his partner had won the first round of clubs he placed the declarer with Jxx. He discarded two diamonds on the second and third hearts, and on the fourth heart he had to part with his winning spade. Now Zorlu, a tempo ahead, played a diamond. South exited with a club, won in dummy, and another diamond left East with two winning jacks. It was a hard won 6 IMPs. Britain won the match after a close struggle.

*Tony Forrester contemplates the defence.*

# Poland v. Israel

The Poles, who had had a hard battle against Finland in the first round, soon struck a heavy blow.

*East-West game; Dealer South.*

```
                    ♠K3
                    ♡KJ98764
                    ◇Q5
                    ♣107
        ♠8752                       ♠A964
        ♡Q103         N             ♡5
        ◇642        W   E           ◇10873
        ♣653          S             ♣Q942
                    ♠QJ10
                    ♡A2
                    ◇AKJ9
                    ♣AKJ8
```

**Closed room**

| West | North | East | South |
|------|-------|------|-------|
| *Rand* | *Martens* | *Friedman* | *Szymanowski* |
| | | | 1 ♣ |
| Pass | 1 ◇ | Pass | 2 NT |
| Pass | 4 ◇ | Pass | 4 NT |
| Pass | 5 ◇ | Pass | 6 NT |
| All Pass | | | |

It looks as though North's four diamonds was a transfer showing long hearts. In 6NT a spade was led to the ace and East returned a diamond. The declarer won in dummy and tested the hearts with the ace and king. He still had time (since the king of spades was still in dummy) to pick up four tricks in clubs.

There is another line of play in 6NT. When Robson, for Britain, was declarer the defence began with a spade to the ace and a spade back. Hoping to gain some information, Robson played off four rounds of diamonds. The result was that when he played ace and king of hearts he lacked a vital entry to pick up the necessary four tricks in clubs.

One other point: when East wins the first trick with the ace of spades his best return is a club, which South is sure to win with the ace.

*Marek Szymanowski of Poland.*

**Open room**

| West | North | East | South |
|------|-------|------|-------|
| *Lasocki* | *Altshuler* | *Gawrys* | *Kaufman* |
| | | | 2 ♣ |
| Pass | 2 ♦ | Pass | 2 NT |
| Pass | 4 ♦ | Pass | 4 ♥ |
| Pass | 4 NT | Pass | 5 ♣ |
| Pass | 6 ♥ | All Pass | |

West led a spade to the ace and a spade came back. South misguessed the trumps and the Poles gained 1040, which is 15 IMPs. They continued to play a fine game, winning 25–5.

# Germany v. Italy

Weak third hand openings are tricky when you are playing the canapé style. The Germans dug a deep pit for themselves on this deal:

*East-West game; Dealer East.*

```
              ♠ Q 10 9
              ♡ A Q 3 2
              ◇ A Q 9 7
              ♣ 10 2
♠ A J 2              ┌─────────┐         ♠ K 6 4
♡ K J 9 7 6         │    N    │         ♡ 5
◇ 10 4 3 2          │ W     E │         ◇ K 8 6 5
♣ 3                 │    S    │         ♣ K J 9 5 4
                    └─────────┘
              ♠ 8 7 5 3
              ♡ 10 8 4
              ◇ J
              ♣ A Q 8 7 6
```

| West | North | East | South |
|------|-------|------|-------|
| *Nippgen* | *Rosati* | *Rohowsky* | *Lauria* |
|  |  | Pass | Pass |
| 1♡ | Pass | 2♣ | Pass |
| Pass | Double | All Pass |  |

West could not consider bidding two diamonds on the second round, because this would have implied longer diamonds than hearts. He might have retreated when the double came round to him — but he didn't.

The play went: spade to the nine and king, heart to jack and queen, low diamond, king from declarer; diamond back, two tricks to North, leaving:

```
              ♠ Q 10
              ♡ A 3 2
              ◇ A
              ♣ 10 2
♠ A J               ┌─────────┐         ♠ 6 4
♡ K 9 7 6           │    N    │         ♡ None
◇ 10                │ W     E │         ◇ 8
♣ 3                 │    S    │         ♣ K J 9 5 4
                    └─────────┘
              ♠ 7 5 3
              ♡ None
              ◇ None
              ♣ A Q 8 7 6
```

South ruffed the fourth diamond and led a spade. Declarer won with the ace and played a club to the jack and queen. Now a spade to the queen, ace of hearts ruffed and overruffed; then the *coup de grâce*, thirteenth spade ruffed by the ten of clubs, promoting two more trump tricks for South. It was 1100 to the Italians and, I dare say, a matter of thought for the Germans.

*Roland Rohowsky listens to an opponent's explanation.*

# Day Two

## Germany v. Italy

Rather bad luck to play in five clubs doubled and make it on a finesse, then find you have dropped six match points. It happened on this deal:

*Love all; Dealer East.*

```
                ♠ A K 6 5 2
                ♡ Q 8 6 5 4 2
                ◇ 9 5
                ♣ None
   ♠ J                              ♠ Q 7 3
   ♡ A K 7          N               ♡ J
   ◇ K Q J 8 3   W     E            ◇ 10 7
   ♣ A 9 8 7        S               ♣ Q J 10 6 4 3 2
                ♠ 10 9 8 4
                ♡ 10 9 3
                ◇ A 6 4 2
                ♣ K 5
```

**Closed room**

| West | North | East | South |
|------|-------|------|-------|
| *Duboin* | *Bittschene* | *Bocchi* | *Ludewig* |
| | | 3♣ | Pass |
| 5♣ | Double | Pass | Pass |
| Redouble | All Pass | | |

Was North's double of five clubs for take-out? Presumably, because it was made without any hesitation. South led the ace of diamonds and followed with a spade. Then East made no mistake in the trump suit. The Italians recorded 800 (400 for tricks, 300 for game, 100 for a redoubled contract made).

**Open room**

| West | North | East | South |
|------|-------|------|-------|
| *Nippgen* | *Rosatil* | *Rohowsky* | *Lauria* |
| | | 2 NT | Pass |
| 3♣ | 4♣ | Pass | 4♠ |
| 5♣ | Pass | Pass | Double |
| All Pass | | | |

East's 2NT signified a pre-empt in *any* suit. North led a high spade and switched to a diamond. West took the trump finesse to score 550 and may have been disappointed to lose 6 IMPs.

---

## Overheard at the bookstall

"Do you have any basic books on opening leads? It's for my partner."

# Germany v. Italy (second half)

Since this book is entitled 'Brilliancies and Blunders' we are forced, reluctantly, to give the occasional blunders an innings.

*Love all; Dealer North.*

```
                    ♠ K 8 5
                    ♡ K 6 5
                    ◇ Q 9 6 4
                    ♣ J 7 6
    ♠ A J 3         ┌─────────┐      ♠ 10
    ♡ A Q 10 9 7    │    N    │      ♡ J 2
    ◇ 5             │ W     E │      ◇ K J 7 3
    ♣ 10 9 8 2      │    S    │      ♣ A K Q 5 4 3
                    └─────────┘
                    ♠ Q 9 7 6 4 2
                    ♡ 8 4 3
                    ◇ A 10 8 2
                    ♣ None
```

The usual contract on this deal was six clubs by East, and the usual result one down. In the open room, for example, a spade was led against Italy's six clubs. The declarer won with the ace, drew trumps, and took the heart finesse. North then led a diamond and the players put their cards back in the boards, recording 50 to North-South.

But you never know at this game. Ludewig played from the West side in six clubs, after one of those auctions where it wasn't easy to tell how the cards were lying. Versini, North, led a spade to the queen and ace. Declarer drew trumps, then ran the jack of hearts to North's king. Seeing no particular danger, North exited with a low spade. Well, there's not much difference between going one down and two down in a slam, so Ludewig let this run to the jack — and all dummy's diamonds went away.

At some tables West played this hand in four hearts — generally when South had overcalled the opening bid with a fairly revolting three spades. It's not impossible to go down now. Say that North leads a spade to the queen and ace. West may ruff a spade, then run the jack of hearts to North's king. Now club ruff, spade to the king, club ruff and ace of diamonds is *two* down, and that was the score at one table.

---

"The good-looking fellow," said Monty Rosenberg, introducing the Irish players on Bridgerama, "is Rory Boland, sitting West. East is Pat Walshe, but you can only see the back of his head. Probably his best view," Monty added.

*A rapt Bridgerama audience.*

# Britain v. Spain

Suppose that you reach a somewhat unsound six hearts with the following cards:

*East-West game; Dealer East.*

♠ A Q J 10 7
♡ K 8 7 6 5
◇ A J 4
♣ None

♠ 3 led

```
      N
  W       E
      S
```

♠ K 8 4
♡ J 10 9 4 3
◇ Q 7 6 5
♣ J

| West | North | East | South |
|------|-------|------|-------|
|      | *Robson* |   | *Forrester* |
|      |       | 1♣ | 1♡ |
| Pass | 6♡ | All Pass | |

Not much of a one heart overcall, but there it is, your partner has raised you to six and West leads a spade. If you play low from dummy you can win with the eight. How do you set about the play?

It's not just a matter of finding East with the ace of hearts or Ax. The spades will supply only two discards and in all

*Forrester discussing Robson's bucolic choice of sequence.*

probability East will hold the king of diamonds. (It looks as though West has passed with long clubs and a poor hand.)

Forrester's line was very clever, as you will see in a moment.

```
                 ♠ A Q J 10 7
                 ♡ K 8 7 6 5
                 ♢ A J 4
                 ♣ None
   ♠ 9 5 3         ┌─────────┐      ♠ 6 2
   ♡ Q 2           │    N    │      ♡ A
   ♢ 10 8 3        │ W     E │      ♢ K 9 2
   ♣ Q 10 7 4 2    │    S    │      ♣ A K 9 8 6 5 3
                   └─────────┘
                 ♠ K 8 4
                 ♡ J 10 9 4 3
                 ♢ Q 7 6 5
                 ♣ J
```

The play went: spade to the eight, ruff club, jack and another spade! If East ruffs he is on play. If he discards, then South runs a heart to the ace, and again East is on play. If in either case East exits with a diamond you win in hand with the queen; if with a club, you win in dummy, discarding a diamond. Pretty, isn't it?

## Netherlands v. Denmark

In a technical sense this has been the hand of the tournament so far.

*Love all; Dealer South.*

```
                    ♠ 10964
                    ♡ 8
                    ◇ J76432
                    ♣ K2
        ♠ Q3                          ♠ AK5
        ♡ KQJ654      N              ♡ A1073
        ◇ A10       W   E            ◇ Q9
        ♣ 873         S              ♣ A954
                    ♠ J872
                    ♡ 92
                    ◇ K85
                    ♣ QJ106
```

**Closed room**

| West | North | East | South |
|------|-------|------|-------|
| *Vergoed* | *Dam* | *Tammens* | *Mohr* |
| | | | Pass |
| 1♡ | Pass | 2♣ | Pass |
| 2♡ | Pass | 3♡ | Pass |
| 4◇ | Pass | 4♠ | Pass |
| 5◇ | Pass | 6♡ | All Pass |

Evidently the raise to three hearts was forcing. Most pairs reached the slam.

Suppose that North leads a spade, as he did here. One line for the Dutch declarer is to lead a low club early on. If North fails to play the king (which could be silly) West can go up with the ace, discard a club on the third spade and exit with a club to North's king. North will have to lead a diamond now and West will have to take a view. Vergoed followed this line but misguessed the diamonds.

Arnarson, of Iceland, followed the same general line and made the contract. The French, who were having a bad time in their match, went down after North had led a *low* club. Abécassis read this as a singleton and tried some end-play in diamonds.

In a way, this contract can always be made. Suppose that declarer plays off all the hearts and spades. When he is down to one club and two diamonds in each hand the defenders have to do the same, and then a club forces them to open up the diamonds, which is fatal from either side.

**Open room**
West began with a forcing pass and the Danish pair played in a conservative four hearts, gaining 11 points.

At the end of the second day the scores at the top were extremely close: Poland 82, Britain 81.5, Greece 81, Italy 80, Sweden 77, Iceland 76. If you wonder about that .5, it signified a penalty for slow play in the match against Israel. Yugoslavia has already incurred penalties amounting to 4 VP for 'tardiness', which means late arrival.

# Day Three

## Ireland v. Hungary

There was a hand on Bridgerama that teachers might like to use in an exam to separate the trouts from the minnows.

*Love all; Dealer West.*

```
                    ♠ K Q 5
                    ♡ Q J 8 5 3
                    ◇ A 10 3
                    ♣ 10 6
  ♠ 7 6 4 3                          ♠ A 9 8 2
  ♡ K           ┌─────────┐          ♡ 7 6 4
  ◇ 9 7 5       │   N     │          ◇ J 8 6 2
  ♣ A K J 7 2   │ W   E   │          ♣ 8 4
                │   S     │
                └─────────┘
                    ♠ J 10
                    ♡ A 10 9 2
                    ◇ K Q 4
                    ♣ Q 9 5 3
```

When Hungary was North-South the bidding, for this tournament, was unusually brief: one heart by North, four hearts by South. (Most of the players, I find, are quite incapable of making a sensible response on a good hand.)

East led a club and after making the jack and ace Mesbur switched to a spade. This was good play, because if he plays a third club East will be unable to overruff the dummy and the king of hearts will then be a dead duck.

East took the ace of spades and returned a spade to the king. Now the Open room audience expected the declarer, Gabor Macskassy, to drop the king of hearts with a learned air, but in a sense he did even better: he crossed to dummy with a diamond and led a third club, ruffing with the eight. When East was unable to overruff the position was entirely clear.

You see why the declarer went out of his way to ruff the third round of clubs? If East had followed suit the inference about the king of hearts would no longer have been valid; it would have been sensible play then to take the trump finesse.

At the other table the contract was defeated, but Ireland nevertheless won the match by a big margin.

As you see, the hand gave rise to two testing plays: West's refusal to lead a third round of clubs and declarer's discovery play of a third round of clubs, leading to the eclipse of the king of hearts.

## Ladies Pairs (qualifying round)

I didn't hear about this hand until a day or two later, after I had described some deals from the final. The heroine was Bep Vriend, most famous of all the Dutch ladies. She has won the Dutch pairs championship seven times in the last fifteen years, playing with four different partners.

*Love all; Dealer West.*

```
              ♠ K72
              ♡ Q954
              ◇ K986
              ♣ A9
  ♠ AJ86         N        ♠ 94
  ♡ K        W       E     ♡ 1072
  ◇ A3           S        ◇ Q1072
  ♣ KJ8762                ♣ Q543
              ♠ Q1053
              ♡ AJ863
              ◇ J54
              ♣ 10
```

| West | North | East | South |
|------|-------|------|-------|
| *Nehmert* | *Arnolds* | *Vogt* | *Vriend* |
| 1♣ | Pass | Pass | 1♡ |
| 1♠ | 2♠ | 3♣ | 3♡ |
| Pass | 4♡ | All Pass | |

'As you can see, Arnolds and Vriend don't suffer from high anxiety', remarked the Dutch reporter. Yes, I do see that.

West led a low club to the ace in dummy, and Bep concluded at once that since East evidently held the queen of clubs she could not hold as much as a king outside. Bep therefore banged out the ace of hearts, drew the rest of the trumps, and then led a low diamond from hand.

West was not so indolent as to play low. She went up with the ace and played a second round. Declarer ducked and East came in with the queen of diamonds. East returned the nine of spades (no difference if she plays a diamond at this point), and South went up with the *queen* of spades. Bidding and making four hearts was a clear top.

---

Heard outside the room where this qualifying round was played: "It's so dark in there, you can't even see the cigarette smoke!"

# Ladies Pairs (qualifying round and final)

"Quite clever, but these things never happen in real life" is a comment to which writers on the game are accustomed. But they do, sometimes! These two hands, containing technical moves that I described at least thirty or forty years ago, both turned up in the Ladies Pairs. (I have changed them a little to make South the declarer.)

*North-South game; Dealer South.*

```
              ♠J72
              ♡AQ32
              ◇J
              ♣109875
♠1098654                    ♠A3
♡104          N             ♡J9876
◇1082       W   E           ◇KQ974
♣QJ           S             ♣4
              ♠KQ
              ♡K5
              ◇A653
              ♣AK632
```

Playing in 3NT (six clubs not easy to reach in a pairs), South wins the third diamond and runs the clubs. This is awkward for East, who is threatened in three suits and has to find a discard from ♠A, ◇9 and ♡J987. In such a situation the best discard is a *heart*, the suit held on your right. You surrender one trick, but not two.

The other example is very much the book type.

*Love all; Dealer South.*

```
              ♠973
              ♡AQJ1062
              ◇Q2
              ♣QJ
♠J108                       ♠A4
♡K873         N             ♡54
◇1054       W   E           ◇J93
♣832          S             ♣AK9764
              ♠KQ652
              ♡9
              ◇AK876
              ♣105
```

South was in four spades and the defence began with two top clubs. Knowing that a third club would concede a ruff-and-discard, Vriend led a third club! When she came in later with the ace of spades she played a fourth club, establishing West's jack of spades for the setting trick.

*Rixi Markus, the world's most famous woman player in Killarney as a journalist.*

# Liechtenstein v. Greece

One of the most disconcerting episodes of the championship befell the declarer on this deal:

*Game all; Dealer South.*

```
              ♠ Q 7
              ♡ 10 6 4
              ◇ A K J 10 5 3
              ♣ 8 2
♠ K J 9 8 6 2      ┌─────────┐      ♠ A 4
♡ J 8 3            │    N    │      ♡ 9 5 2
◇ 7 6              │  W   E  │      ◇ Q 9 2
♣ 6 4             │    S    │      ♣ Q J 10 7 5
              └─────────┘
              ♠ 10 5 3
              ♡ A K Q 7
              ◇ 8 4
              ♣ A K 9 3
```

| West | North | East | South |
|------|-------|------|-------|
|      |       |      | 1 NT  |
| Pass | 3 NT  | All Pass |    |

West led the eight of spades, covered by the queen and ace. The declarer must have looked like a man who held K J 10 x or similar, for East, instead of returning a spade, switched to the queen of clubs. South won and led a diamond to the ten. This gave East a chance to defeat the contract by three tricks, but he knew the clever play at this point: noting that dummy held no side entries, he ducked this trick.

South now ran four tricks in hearts, then led his second diamond. When West followed suit he showed his cards and claimed twelve tricks.

"Director!" called the defenders.

The English tournament director, Max Bavin, came to the table and the circumstances were described. "Naturally, I was going to play the ace and king from dummy," declared South.

"Sorry," said Max, "but there was an alternative play. You might have thought that West held four diamonds to the queen and have intended to finesse again. Let me see, in that case the defenders make a diamond and five spades (West had thrown a spade on the fourth heart). Two down, 200 to East-West."

26

## Standings after Round 6 (Day Three)

| | | | | | |
|---|---|---|---|---|---|
| 1. | Great Britain | 120.5 | 14. | Denmark | 92 |
| 2. | Iceland | 119 | 15. | Hungary | 90 |
| 3. | Sweden | 119 | 15. | Turkey | 90 |
| 4. | Italy | 116 | 17. | Ireland | 86 |
| 5. | USSR | 112 | 18. | Czechoslovakia | 79 |
| 6. | France | 110 | 19. | Netherlands | 78 |
| 7. | Poland | 107 | 20. | Spain | 74 |
| 8. | Austria | 101 | 21. | Finland | 73 |
| 9. | Greece | 98 | 22. | Belgium | 71 |
| 9. | Germany | 98 | 23. | Bulgaria | 69.5 |
| 11. | Portugal | 95 | 24. | Liechtenstein | 64.5 |
| 11. | Norway | 95 | 25. | Switzerland | 51 |
| 13. | Israel | 94.5 | 26. | Yugoslavia | 31 |

No great surprises yet, except that the Netherlands supporters are not very pleased with their team's performance. They are sure to improve.

Britain has been playing well but has not so far met any of the top teams. Iceland may not *quite* keep its position. Poland lost quite heavily to Italy but still looks formidable.

The USSR team, playing in the European for the first time, is well placed, but this is no surprise. Their players have done well both in the Cavendish Pairs (New York) and the *Sunday Times*. And after all, they're not bad at chess, are they?

---

### Oh, I don't know

"My husband is the Chief Librarian of the National Library of Scotland," said Liz McGowan (British ladies team) during an interview, "but it's easy to overstate the excitement of that."

# Day Four

## Britain v. Ireland

Roman Smolski, who plays with Tony Sowter, is one of the few mavericks among the top teams. His style of play resembles that of Irving Rose. This was one of his good results:

*Love all; Dealer East.*

```
                 ♠ Q 9 8
                 ♡ A 10 9 5
                 ◇ K 8 6 2
                 ♣ 8 6
  ♠ J 7 6 4                         ♠ 10 5
  ♡ J 8 7 4        N                ♡ Q 6
  ◇ J 9 4 3     W     E             ◇ 10 7
  ♣ 5              S                ♣ A K Q 7 4 3 2
                 ♠ A K 3 2
                 ♡ K 3 2
                 ◇ A Q 5
                 ♣ J 10 9
```

The traditional Acol style is to open 3NT on the East hand. It is a convention I have, perforce, described in books on the system, though I have not a high opinion of it. Smolski chose 1NT and this was the sequence:

| West | North | East | South |
|------|-------|------|-------|
| *Sowter* | *Fitzgibbon* | *Smolski* | *Mesbur* |
| | | 1 NT | Double |
| Redouble | Pass | 2 ♣ | Pass |
| Pass | 3 ♣ | Pass | 3 ♠ |
| Pass | 3 NT | All Pass | |

Sowter's redouble was for a rescue, no doubt, so that East's two clubs did not give the impression of a long suit. Even so, Fitzgibbon's manoeuvres look strange to me. He asks either for a suit or a club guard, and then bids 3NT with nothing in clubs himself.

At the other table the British South played in four spades and Boland began with his singleton club. This seemed all right at first, but when East played three rounds of clubs the discards broke up his partner's hand. The swing was 570, 11 match points to Britain.

On another hand in this match there was much discussion about the best line of play in six hearts on these cards:

| | |
|---|---|
| ♠643 | ♠A872 |
| ♡A987542 | ♡K |
| ◇AK9 | ◇3 |
| ♣None | ♣AKJ10975 |

You win the diamond lead and play a heart to the king. I think that to run the jack of clubs is best. If it holds, ruff the next round and play ace and another heart. This will give you enough tricks, barring accidents.

*Tony Sowter is amused by Smolski's strong no-trump.*

# Britain v. Ireland

Is the 'king of clubs is always single' legend, a firm tradition in Europe, taking a rest? I have already seen three hands where a singleton king of hearts played an important role.

*Love all; Dealer East.*

```
              ♠ A 6 4
              ♡ 8 4
              ◇ J 10 7 3
              ♣ K 10 5 3
♠ Q 10 5                        ♠ 3 2
♡ Q J 10 9 2    ┌─────────┐     ♡ A 7 6 5 3
◇ K 6 5 2       │    N    │     ◇ Q
♣ 6             │  W   E  │     ♣ A Q 9 7 2
                │    S    │
                └─────────┘
              ♠ K J 9 8 7
              ♡ K
              ◇ A 9 8 4
              ♣ J 8 4
```

At both tables the bidding was on simple lines:

| West | North | East | South |
|------|-------|------|-------|
|      |       | 1♡   | 1♠    |
| 4♡   | All Pass |   |       |

Both South players led a club from their unattractive holding, and at trick two both declarers advanced the singleton queen of diamonds. Kirby followed with the *jack* under the ace, with the idea of advising partner to switch hastily to a spade. Armstrong thought his partner was showing an odd number and played another diamond, which wasn't great for his side.

At the other table Mesbur led a spade after the ace of diamonds and all depended now on the play in the trump suit. Before the amusing and learned commentator (Ron Andersen, from America) had got far in his analysis, Robson banged out the ace. North had already shown the ace of spades and the king of clubs.

---

### Good sign

"Will you be going to the golf (the Carrolls tournament) tomorrow?" one of the locals asked a friend at the bar. "Maybe. The rain today was much warmer than yesterday."

*The Irish scoring up.*

# Britain v. Ireland

*A rush to get the results in the press room.*

An old friend and colleague, Jean Besse, of Switzerland, analysed this hand in a way that others missed.

*Love all; Dealer East.*

                    ♠ J 4 3
                    ♡ A Q 9
                    ◇ A 9 7 6 5
                    ♣ A 2
    ♠ 9 5                           ♠ A K Q 10 8 6
    ♡ 8 7 6 5 4     N               ♡ K J
    ◇ 10          W   E             ◇ K Q J 4 2
    ♣ J 10 9 6 5    S               ♣ None
                    ♠ 7 2
                    ♡ 10 3 2
                    ◇ 8 3
                    ♣ K Q 8 7 4 3

| West | North | East | South |
|------|-------|------|-------|
| *Sowter* | *Walshe* | *Smolski* | *Boland* |
|      |       | 2♠ | Pass |
| 3♣ | Double | 3◇ | Pass |
| 3♠ | Pass | 4♠ | All Pass |

West's three clubs, in response to the opening two bid, was a negative.

South made a good lead against four spades, the two of trumps. Dummy played the five and North covered with the jack — a small error, because it allowed East an entry to dummy for a heart to the king and jack.

Suppose that North does not contribute the jack of spades. East has to win and lead a diamond to the ten and ace. North then plays the jack of spades, so that dummy will never gain the lead. Declarer will play trumps now, leading to this position:

```
              ♠ None
              ♡ A Q
              ♢ 9 7 6 5
              ♣ A 2
 ♠ None                      ♠ 8 6
 ♡ 8 7 6         N           ♡ K J
 ♢ None       W     E        ♢ K Q J 4
 ♣ J 10 9 6 5    S           ♣ None
              ♠ None
              ♡ 10 3 2
              ♢ 8
              ♣ K Q 8 7
```

On the next spade North must discard — the ace of clubs! If the last spade follows, he can afford to throw the queen of hearts.

In better form than usual against the old rivals, Britain won 23–7.

# Sweden v. Germany

Most of the Swedish pairs, particularly Fallenius and Nilsland, play a fairly incomprehensible system. Their opponents in this match, Splettstösser and Häusler, worked hard on their counter-measures, with interesting results on occasions.

*Mats Nilsland suffering at the hands of the Germans.*

*East-West game; Dealer East.*

```
              ♠842
              ♡A86
              ◇A7
              ♣AJ952
♠106                        ♠AKJ75
♡1095        ┌─N──┐        ♡J74
◇1082       W│    │E       ◇Q53
♣KQ764       └─S──┘        ♣108
              ♠Q93
              ♡KQ32
              ◇KJ964
              ♣3
```

What would you expect the final contract to be? Even with knowledge of the Swedish system you would hardly guess.

| West | North | East | South |
|------|-------|------|-------|
| *Fallenius* | *Splettstösser* | *Nilsland* | *Häusler* |
| | | 1 ♠ [1] | Double [2] |
| Pass | Pass [3] | Pass | |

[1] Promising 8 to 13 points and at least three cards in spades.

[2] Either 11–15 with at least three cards in both majors or any 16+.

[3] 'Taking a view'. East might have held fewer spades and might have moved into still deeper waters. In any case, North-South will have at least six spades between them.

Nilsland, with five good spades, was probably content, but if so he was soon to be disappointed. The defence was deadly: club to ace, three rounds of diamonds, king and another heart, club ruff; heart ruff (North had thrown one earlier), and another club, promoting South's queen of spades. That was 800 to set against 460 at the other table, a swing of eight points to Germany.

I don't want to 'hammer' this business of artificial systems, but one point does occur to me. At present the motive is usually to improve the bidding of your own side. This may change to devising systems that are purely obstructive. If so, the game will become a test of inventor's ingenuity.

# Britain v. France

This is usually one of the big matches of the championship, but it came a little too early for that. Besides, most of the attention was concentrated on the following episode.

*North-South game; Dealer West.*

```
                ♠ Q 10 5
                ♡ 9 3
                ◇ Q J 9 8 7 6 3
                ♣ 6
    ♠ J 3 2         ┌─────────┐        ♠ 9 7 6 4
    ♡ Q 5 4 2       │    N    │        ♡ A 10 8 6
    ◇ 10 5 4        │ W     E │        ◇ 2
    ♣ J 7 5         │    S    │        ♣ Q 10 9 8
                    └─────────┘
                ♠ A K 8
                ♡ K J 7
                ◇ A K
                ♣ A K 4 3 2
```

**Closed room**

| West | North | East | South |
|------|-------|------|-------|
|      | *Robson* |    | *Forrester* |
| Pass | Pass | Pass | 2♣ |
| Pass | 4♠ | Pass | 4 NT |
| Pass | 5◇ | Pass | 5 NT |
| Pass | 6◇ | All Pass | |

In some sequences a bid of spades is a transfer to diamonds but Forrester was not entirely sure what was happening. His bids of 4NT and 5NT were of an interrogative nature and he was content to pass six diamonds. After a trump lead there were 13 tricks.

**Open room**

| West | North | East | South |
|------|-------|------|-------|
|      | *Quantin* |    | *Abécassis* |
|      | Pass | Pass | 2◇ |
| Pass | 2♡ | Pass | 2 NT |
| Pass | 4◇ | Pass | 5♠ |
| Pass | 6◇ | Pass | 6♠ |
| All Pass | | | |

This went four down, just about the margin of Britain's 18–12 victory.

When one of the French supporters said later to Abécassis "I hear you played a slam in the wrong suit," he replied with dignity, "They were both no-loser suits."

*Europe's highest ranked Junior Jean-Christophe Quantin.*

# Ireland v. Czechoslovakia

There was some pretty, if not entirely sound, play and counter-play on this deal:

*North-South game; Dealer West.*

```
              ♠QJ1075
              ♡AK432
              ◇AQ
              ♣J
  ♠9842           N          ♠AK6
  ♡J1085      W     E        ♡97
  ◇1072          S           ◇86
  ♣94                        ♣AQ10873
              ♠3
              ♡Q6
              ◇KJ9543
              ♣K652
```

With Ireland East-West the bidding went:

| West | North | East | South |
|------|-------|------|-------|
| *Scannell* | *Fort* | *Brennan* | *Illa* |
| Pass | 1♠ | 3♣ | Pass |
| Pass | 4♡ | All Pass | |

North's four hearts was decidedly venturesome, in my opinion. He was lucky to find such useful support.

East began with the nine of hearts, as no doubt the declarer would be aiming to ruff spades. The first question is, how should declarer plan the early play?

Tomas Fort made a surprising play that looks pretty good: he ducked the first trick, letting the nine of hearts hold. Obviously if trumps are continued he will have good chances to land eleven tricks.

What should East do next? He made what the Bulletin reporter called a 'subtle switch' to the eight of diamonds. This was surprisingly, almost unforeseeably, awkward for the declarer. Because of the entry situation he had to take the ace of diamonds and play ace and king of hearts, crashing the queen. When the trumps did not divide, he was set to go at least one down.

Another defence, after the nine of hearts, would also have succeeded. If East cashes his two aces and then plays the king of spades, forcing dummy's queen of hearts, he will establish a second trump trick for his side.

# Ladies Pairs final

David Greenwood, a former English international who at present lives in Ireland, showed me a fine hand from the pairs final.

*East-West game; Dealer North.*

```
              ♠ A Q 2
              ♡ 8
              ◇ K Q J 7 6 5 3 2
              ♣ Q
  ♠ 5                      ♠ J 8 7 3
  ♡ 10 9 4      N          ♡ K 5 3 2
  ◇ 10 9      W   E        ◇ A 8
  ♣ A K J 10 6 5 4  S      ♣ 9 8 7
              ♠ K 10 9 6 4
              ♡ A Q J 7 6
              ◇ 4
              ♣ 3 2
```

South was Dominique Joegre, one of the many French players who dominated this event. The bidding went:

| West | North | East | South |
|------|-------|------|-------|
|      | 1 ◇   | Pass | 1 ♠   |
| 3 ♣  | 3 ◇   | 4 ♣  | 4 ♡   |
| Pass | 4 ♠   | All Pass |    |

Digressing for a moment, I wonder why almost all players make bids like West's three clubs. It is certain that her side is going to be outbid, so what is the point of giving the opponents information that may well be useful to them?

West led the ace of clubs and followed with the king. As South, how would you plan the play?

With scarcely a moment's thought the declarer discarded dummy's singleton heart! Obviously, if dummy's trumps are shortened South will have to say good-bye to the long diamonds.

Now consider the affair from West's angle. It looked as though South was aiming to bring in the diamonds. Placing her partner with the ace of hearts, she led a heart, which ran to South's queen. A diamond lost to the ace and East now played her third club. Declarer ruffed in hand, played a spade to the ace, and ran the diamonds. East could only choose the moment to concede the remainder.

Note that it would not have been right for declarer to cash the second high spade in dummy. East then ruffs the third round of diamonds and South is left with a losing heart at the finish.

# Day Five

## Britain v. Poland

The British team didn't do many clever things against Poland, but one of them occurred on this deal:

*Love all; Dealer North.*

♠ J 10 9 2
♡ A Q 10 8 3
◇ 9 2
♣ 5 3

♣ 2 led

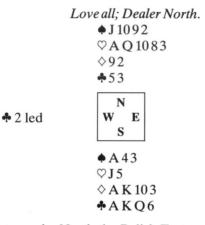

♠ A 4 3
♡ J 5
◇ A K 10 3
♣ A K Q 6

After a pass by North the Polish East opened one spade. In ten years you wouldn't guess what this signified: it meant that he had a count of 0–8 and that his spades numbered 0, 1, 2, or 6.

South doubled and finished in 3NT. West led a club to the seven and king. There are eight tricks on top (since you can rely on at least two tricks in hearts), but where do you go for the ninth?

Armstrong found a line that is simple but eluded the commentators among others. He began with ace and another spade. This was the full hand:

```
                    ♠ J 10 9 2
                    ♡ A Q 10 8 3
                    ◇ 9 2
                    ♣ 5 3
    ♠ Q 8 7 5            N            ♠ K 6
    ♡ 6 4          W         E        ♡ K 9 7 2
    ◇ J 8 7 5           S            ◇ Q 6 4
    ♣ J 4 2                          ♣ 10 9 8 7
                    ♠ A 4 3
                    ♡ J 5
                    ◇ A K 10 3
                    ♣ A K Q 6
```

When he won the second spade East returned a club. Now South led the jack of hearts, an essential move at this point. When East held off, South reverted to spades, with the ace of hearts as an entry for the fourth spade.

At the other table South was not tested because West began with a low diamond, ensuring three diamond tricks for the declarer. It was that sort of match. Poland won 22–8.

---

### Oh, I don't know

"My husband is the Chief Librarian of the National Library of Scotland," said Liz McGowan (British ladies team) during an interview, "but it's easy to overstate the excitement of that."

# Ladies Pairs final

*Sandra Penfold of Great Britain.*

See if you can attach your mind to this little problem. North, the dummy, and East hold:

*East-West game; Dealer West.*

        ♠ 4
        ♡ K J 9 8
        ◇ 6 2
        ♣ Q J 10 8 6 4

                        ♠ K J 107
                        ♡ A 3
    ◇ 3 led    W  E     ◇ A J 104
                        ♣ 7 5 2

The bidding has been:

| West | North | East | South |
|------|-------|------|-------|
| Pass | Pass | 1◇ | Double |
| Pass | 2♡ | Pass | 2♠ |
| Pass | 3♣ | Pass | 3NT |
| All Pass | | | |

West might have led low from Qxx, but South has done a good bit of bidding and is likely to hold a double stop in diamonds. So how do you defend? It looks right to win with the ace of diamonds and switch to the jack of spades. This will produce five tricks if West has the queen of spades.

West did have the queen of spades, so this defence was good enough for one down. But East can do better, as you will see from the diagram:

```
              ♠4
              ♡KJ98
              ◇62
              ♣QJ10864
♠Q82          ┌─────────┐    ♠KJ107
♡Q10752       │   N     │    ♡A3
◇973          │ W   E   │    ◇AJ104
♣93           │   S     │    ♣752
              └─────────┘
              ♠A9653
              ♡64
              ◇KQ85
              ♣AK
```

South, who has doubled the opening bid and has not supported the hearts or clubs, is in all probability 5–2–4–2. So, what about killing the dummy by returning a *low* heart? Judy Norris, of Denmark, did just this, for two down. Add this deal to the one just shown, and never join those who say 'The women don't bid badly but they can't play the cards'.

# Ladies Pairs final

This was a neat hand from the final round:

*Love all; Dealer South.*

```
                ♠ K 103
                ♡ K J 10
                ◇ A K 6
                ♣ K 865
   ♠ A 72                      ♠ Q J 9854
   ♡ Q 763        N           ♡ A 8
   ◇ Q 542     W     E        ◇ J 10
   ♣ 94           S           ♣ A J 10
                ♠ 6
                ♡ 9542
                ◇ 9873
                ♣ Q 732
```

| West | North | East | South |
|------|-------|------|-------|
|      |       |      | Pass  |
| Pass | 1 NT  | 2 ♠  | All Pass |

South led a low club to the king and ace. At trick two the declarer . . .

You didn't stop me? The declarer (sorry, my informant could not tell me her name) *ducked* the first club. She won the second round and advanced the jack of diamonds. South was never able to gain the lead and play a heart, so East made nine tricks, losing just one spade, two diamonds and one club.

*Sabine Zenkel of Germany.*

There were nine French pairs in the 28-pairs final. The leading scores in the Coriandre European Ladies Pairs Championship were:

| | | | |
|---|---|---|---|
| 1. | Chevalley – Avon | France | 160.92 |
| 2. | Nehmert – Vogt | Germany | 160.27 |
| 3. | Fraser – Stiefsohn | Austria | 158.78 |
| 4. | Von Armin – Zenkel | Germany | 158.38 |
| 5. | Sanders – Harper | Britain | 157.68 |
| 6. | Zorlu - Taner | Turkey | 157.03 |
| 7. | Midskog – Landstrom | Sweden | 155.27 |
| 8. | Arnolds – Vriend | Netherlands | 154.78 |
| 9. | Van der Pas – Schippers | Netherlands | 154.10 |
| 10. | Bourchtoff – Girardin | France | 153.50 |

A good mix. Ginette Chevalley, alongside the two Dutch pairs, was one of the big names in this field. I found out one other thing. "She is almost your age," someone said to me. In that case, *bien joué!*

# Iceland v. Austria

"Austria's not doing particularly well so far," I remarked to somebody. "They've got a young team this year." "Young? I must have played against Babsch at least twenty years ago." "It's his son." That explains it. I had been shown this deal.

*Love all; Dealer South.*

```
                 ♠ A K J 8 3
                 ♡ A 9 4
                 ◇ A K Q 7 2
                 ♣ None
  ♠ Q 6 4 2        ┌─────────┐      ♠ 10 7
  ♡ K 8 5          │   N     │      ♡ J 7 6 3 2
  ◇ None           │ W   E   │      ◇ J 9 8 5
  ♣ A Q 8 5 3 2    │   S     │      ♣ 7 4
                   └─────────┘
                 ♠ 9 5
                 ♡ Q 10
                 ◇ 10 6 4 3
                 ♣ K J 1 0 9 6
```

After West, playing a one club system, had opened a catch-all one diamond, North (Babsch junior) became the declarer in six diamonds. East struck a heart lead, not very good for his side, and dummy's ten was covered by the king and ace. Declarer cashed the ace of diamonds, finding the bad news, then played a heart to the queen, followed by a spade to the ace, heart ruff, king of spades and a spade ruff. The position now was:

```
                 ♠ J 8
                 ♡ None
                 ◇ K Q 7 2
                 ♣ None
  ♠ Q              ┌─────────┐      ♠ None
  ♡ None           │   N     │      ♡ J
  ◇ None           │ W   E   │      ◇ J 9 8
  ♣ A Q 8 5 2      │   S     │      ♣ 7 4
                   └─────────┘
                 ♠ None
                 ♡ None
                 ◇ 10
                 ♣ K J 1 0 9 6
```

At this point you can ruff a club and ruff a spade, but you can get back to the North hand only with a club ruff, and then the defenders will win the last two tricks.

The point to observe in good time here is that when you have found the trumps 4–0 you may need the spade finesse. Ruffing three times leaves you in the predicament shown above. Undoubtedly you must take the spade finesse, bearing in mind that West is void of diamonds and has opened the bidding.

---

### Transfer bid

The Israelis have proposed a transfer to their Irish hosts: You take 25% of our June sunshine and we will take 25% of your June rain.

---

*The victorious Austrian ladies' team: top – Gabi Bamberger, Ernst Pichler (npc), Renata Fraser and Terry Weigkricht; bottom – Helga Stiefsohn, Doris Fischer and Maria Erhart.*

# Ladies Pairs Championship

Chris Dixon, who is captaining the British ladies team, showed me a hand that has one fairly familiar solution, and one that is difficult.

*Game all; Dealer South.*

```
              ♠ Q J 8
              ♡ J 10 8
              ◇ 9 6 4 2
              ♣ 8 5 2
  ♠ 9 4 2          N          ♠ K 10 7 5
  ♡ 9 6 3      W     E        ♡ 5 2
  ◇ K Q 10 5       S          ◇ A J 8 7 3
  ♣ J 10 4                    ♣ Q 7
              ♠ A 6 3
              ♡ A K Q 7 4
              ◇ None
              ♣ A K 9 6 3
```

If you happen to finish in six clubs you must hope that the clubs are 3–2 and that the player who has three clubs also has three hearts; and of course you will need the spade finesse. The play is to ruff the diamond lead, cash two clubs, cross to the jack of hearts and finesse in spades. Then continue hearts, discarding a spade from dummy when eventually West ruffs.

Six hearts may look impossible even at double dummy. First, you must ruff the diamond lead with the queen of hearts. Follow with ace, king and another club. The defence will probably play another diamond (though a trump is better). Again you ruff high, reaching this position:

```
              ♠ Q J 8
              ♡ J 10 8
              ◇ 9 6
              ♣ None
  ♠ 9 4 2          N          ♠ K 10 7 5
  ♡ 9 6 3      W     E        ♡ 5 2
  ◇ Q 10           S          ◇ A 8
  ♣ None                      ♣ None
              ♠ A 6 3
              ♡ A 7 4
              ◇ None
              ♣ 9 6
```

Now a low heart to the ten, ruff a diamond with the ace, finesse the eight of hearts, and draw the last trump. Take the spade finesse and accept congratulations from all sides.

*Britain's Nicola Smith.*

# Iceland v. Austria

A lead through dummy's K Q J x of a side suit, when the declarer is void, is usually fatal for the defence. But see what happened on this occasion.

*Love all; Dealer West.*

```
              ♠ A Q 7 5 3
              ♡ K Q 2
              ◇ K Q J 8
              ♣ 2
  ♠ 8 6 4 2        N          ♠ K 10 9
  ♡ 10 5 4 3    W     E       ♡ 9
  ◇ 6 5 4          S          ◇ A 10 9 7 3 2
  ♣ K 8                       ♣ 9 4 3
              ♠ J
              ♡ A J 8 7 6
              ◇ None
              ♣ A Q J 10 7 6 5
```

Most teams played in six hearts or six clubs, but one or two, including Terraneo for Austria, attempted seven hearts.

After the commentators had spoken their piece West led a diamond, to great cheers from the Northern supporters. You can see that if South ruffs and plays ace and another club, ruffing, the best he can do is overtake the second heart and go one down.

There was then quite an argument about South's chances if instead he plays for a cross-ruff. Monty Rosenberg, from the commentator's bench, wagered that it could be done. Diamond ruffed, spade to the ace, two diamonds cashed, spade ruff, club ace and ruff, spade ruff, leads to:

```
              ♠ Q 7
              ♡ K Q
              ◇ 8
              ♣ None
  ♠ 8              N          ♠ None
  ♡ 10 5 4 3    W     E       ♡ 9
  ◇ None           S          ◇ 10 9 7
  ♣ None                      ♣ 9
              ♠ None
              ♡ A J
              ◇ None
              ♣ J 10 7
```

50

South leads a club and if West fails to ruff the last four tricks are there on a cross-ruff. So West must ruff and dummy over-ruffs. Now, if declarer could cash the queen of spades he would be home, but East is there with his singleton trump. Pity!

---

*Joe Moran, President of the Irish Bridge Union.*

# Ireland v. France (ladies teams)

I am describing more hands from the ladies events than I expected, but then they play so well! (Also, they will have finished their team event before the men.) This is a pretty hand played by Evelyn Bourke, of Ireland.

*Evelyn Bourke.*

*North-South game; Dealer West.*

```
              ♠ K J 7 2
              ♡ 10 4 2
              ♢ J 3
              ♣ A Q 8 6
                    ┌─────┐
                    │  N  │
   ♡ 3 led          │ W  E│
                    │  S  │
                    └─────┘
              ♠ Q 4
              ♡ A K
              ♢ K Q 9 8 2
              ♣ K 10 7 4
```

| West | North | East | South |
|------|-------|------|-------|
| Pass | Pass | 1♡ | 1NT |
| Pass | 2♣ | Pass | 3NT |
| All Pass | | | |

East plays low on the heart lead (no need to sacrifice an honour) and South wins. How should she continue?

Assuming that the clubs are not too hostile, you can see eight tricks on top. If you play a low diamond to the jack East may win and clear the hearts. Now, if the diamonds don't break, you won't have time to make any tricks in spades. The Bourke solution was to enter dummy and play a diamond from the table. This was the full hand:

```
                    ♠ K J 7 2
                    ♡ 10 4 2
                    ◇ J 3
                    ♣ A Q 8 6
  ♠ A 9 8 6          ┌─────────┐        ♠ 10 5 3
  ♡ J 9 3            │    N    │        ♡ Q 8 7 6 5
  ◇ 10 7 6 4         │ W     E │        ◇ A 5
  ♣ 5 2              │    S    │        ♣ J 9 3
                    └─────────┘
                    ♠ Q 4
                    ♡ A K
                    ◇ K Q 9 8 2
                    ♣ K 10 7 4
```

East's one heart was psychic, as you see, but this made no difference to the play. If East goes up with the ace of diamonds South has four tricks in the suit. If East ducks, then South makes a trick with the queen and turns hastily to the spades, making two spades, two hearts, one diamond and four clubs.

# Spain v. Bulgaria

The Spanish South on the deal below was one of a number who played the North-South hands in a spade part-score. It was the sort of hand one gives to a moderately advanced student.

*North-South game; Dealer South.*

```
              ♠ Q 10 9 7
              ♡ J 8 5
              ◇ J 8 4
              ♣ J 6 5
  ♠ 4 3                       ♠ 5 2
  ♡ 10 7 3      N            ♡ Q 9 6 4
  ◇ K 5 2     W   E          ◇ A 10 6 3
  ♣ K 10 8 4 2    S          ♣ A Q 3
              ♠ A K J 8 6
              ♡ A K 2
              ◇ Q 9 7
              ♣ 9 7
```

South plays in three spades and the defence begins with three rounds of clubs, South ruffing. When the trumps fall 2–2 there is a baby elimination: play off ace, king and another heart, forcing the defenders to open up the diamonds. One down, but the best you can do.

At the other table a Bulgarian player, Roumen Mantchev, was confronted by a rather similar problem.

```
              ♠ Q 10 9 7
              ♡ J 8 5
              ◇ J 8 4
              ♣ J 6 5
  ♠ 4 3                       ♠ 5 2
  ♡ 10 7 3      N            ♡ Q 9 6 4
  ◇ K 5 2     W   E          ◇ A 10 6 3
  ♣ K 10 8 4 2    S          ♣ A Q 3
              ♠ A K J 8 6
              ♡ A K
              ◇ Q 9 7
              ♣ 9 7
```

Playing in the same contract of three spades, he ruffed the third club, cashed the ace of spades and ace and king of hearts, crossed to the queen of spades and ruffed the last heart. Now he took the wrong view in diamonds to go one off; really bad luck.

It was realised that something had gone wrong and the tournament director was summoned. Mantchev was awarded a couple of unwelcome presents: the missing two of hearts and a two-trick penalty for the revoke.

# Day Six

## Britain v. Italy

This match against the old rivals followed a strange course. Italy went ahead by 17–0 early on, but then came a series of competitive deals where Italy had the worse of the luck.

*Game all; Dealer West.*

```
                    ♠ K852
                    ♡ A92
                    ◇ None
                    ♣ A Q 10 8 4 2
        ♠ QJ          ┌─────┐        ♠ A 9 7 6 3
        ♡ K3          │  N  │        ♡ Q J 10 8 4
        ◇ AQJ76543    │W   E│        ◇ 108
        ♣ 9           │  S  │        ♣ 5
                      └─────┘
                    ♠ 104
                    ♡ 765
                    ◇ K92
                    ♣ KJ763
```

| West | North | East | South |
|------|-------|------|-------|
| *Sowter* | *Rosati* | *Smolski* | *Lauria* |
| 1◇ | 2♣ | 2♠ | 4♣ |
| 5◇ | All Pass | | |

With both finesses right, Sowter had no problem in his five diamond contract; 600 to Britain.

At the other table Duboin bid only four diamonds on the second round, which seems reasonable. So the bidding went:

| West | North | East | South |
|------|-------|------|-------|
| *Duboin* | *Robson* | *Bocchi* | *Forrester* |
| 1◇ | 2♣ | 2♠ | 4♣ |
| 4◇ | 5♣ | Double | All Pass |

East led the queen of hearts and West had a problem whether or not to overtake with the king. He decided against it and the queen was allowed to hold. Robson took the second heart, played a club to dummy and ruffed a diamond, led another club and ruffed a second diamond. It looks as though the elimination play is going well, but if declarer crosses to dummy to ruff the third diamond he will find that he has run out of trumps in his own hand.

The only chance, therefore, was to play West for an eight-card suit. North exited with his third heart and saved a trick when East had to lead a spade or concede a ruff-and-discard. That was 200 to East-West and nine match points to Britain.

---

*Screens were used throughout this championship and are shown here in the Britain v. Greece match.*

# Britain v. Italy

There was one big swing in the second half. If you had contracted for seven hearts, how would you play as South?

*Love all; Dealer South.*

♠AQJ64
♡QJ87
◇AKJ8
♣None

♠ 2 led

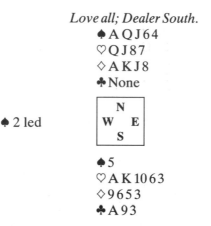

♠5
♡AK1063
◇9653
♣A93

You have opened one heart, North has responded one spade (the fashion in these days — players force only if they have an aunt in China) and East has bid a pre-emptive three clubs. Seven hearts is not going to be easy and you have a critical decision to make on the first trick when West leads a low spade.

Nobody likes to put a grand slam at risk on the opening lead. Furthermore, even if you finesse the queen of spades and it wins the trick, you are not home: unless the spades are lucky you will still need a diamond finesse at some point.

On the whole I think it's right to go up with the ace of spades. If that was your opinion too you will have no cause to regret it, for the full hand was:

```
              ♠AQJ64
              ♡QJ87
              ◇AKJ8
              ♣None
♠1098732                    ♠K
♡5          N               ♡942
◇Q104    W     E            ◇72
♣752        S               ♣KQJ10864
              ♠5
              ♡AK1063
              ◇9653
              ♣A93
```

58

The Italians were in seven and South did the right thing, going up with the ace of spades. Even so, there are only just thirteen tricks on top — five hearts, three spades, two diamonds, ace of clubs and two ruffs. Britain played in six hearts; even if you finesse in spades you still make this.

Britain had led by 69 points at half time and won the match 24–6.

# Ireland v. Finland (ladies teams)

On board four of this match the Irish combination of Aileen and Rosamond O'Keefe bid seven hearts and made it. At the other table Parviainen and Vaaranen stopped in five hearts — were doubled and went one down. This is the story of that strange result.

*Game all; Dealer West.*

```
              ♠ None
              ♡ A K J 10 8
              ◇ Q
              ♣ Q J 10 7 6 4 3
  ♠ A Q 6 5 3            ♠ J 10 8 7 4
  ♡ None      N          ♡ 9 6 5 4
  ◇ J 9 4 3  W   E       ◇ 7 2
  ♣ A 9 8 5      S       ♣ K 2
              ♠ K 9 2
              ♡ Q 7 3 2
              ◇ A K 10 8 6 5
              ♣ None
```

**Open room**

| West | North | East | South |
|------|-------|------|-------|
| *Groneoss* | *A. O'Keefe* | *Hemila* | *R. O'Keefe* |
| 1♠ | 2NT | Pass | 4♡ |
| Pass | 4NT | Pass | 5◇ |
| Pass | 6♡ | 6♠ | Pass |
| Pass | 7♡ | All Pass | |

I don't profess to understand *all* these bids, but there it is, the contract was reasonable. West, who perhaps also missed certain valuable hints, led the ace of clubs; 2210 to Ireland.

**Closed room**

| West | North | East | South |
|------|-------|------|-------|
| *Bourke* | *Parviainen* | *Sloan* | *Vaaranen* |
| 1♠ | 2♣ | 2♠ | 3◇ |
| 3♠ | 4♡ | 4♠ | Double |
| Pass | 5♣ | Pass | Pass |
| Double | Pass | Pass | 5♡ |
| Pass | Pass | Double | All Pass |

South's pass of five clubs seems to indicate a degree of mistrust, but the rest of the bidding was sensible.

A spade lead against five hearts doubled would have allowed eleven tricks on a cross-ruff. But Diane Sloan led a trump. The game now was to set up the clubs — it can be done — but the declarer attempted to cash three diamonds before cross-ruffing and found herself a trick short. It was a swing of 20 IMPs, quite a rarity.

*Diane Sloan of Ireland.*

# Denmark v. Spain

Sometimes there's no justice. Would you rather play these
North-South hands in six clubs or 6NT?

```
                        ♠5
                        ♡QJ3
                        ◇AQ54
                        ♣AK1084
                        ┌─────────┐
                        │    N    │
    ♠ 10 led            │  W   E  │
                        │    S    │
                        └─────────┘
                        ♠AQJ6
                        ♡K4
                        ◇KJ6
                        ♣J732
```

It looks as though both contracts will depend on the clubs.
In general, you would prefer to be in no-trumps. It will be
worth two match points more than six clubs and is proof against
any disaster such as a heart ruff. But see what happened when
the Danes were in 6NT and the Spanish in six clubs.

*East-West game; Dealer West.*

```
                        ♠5
                        ♡QJ3
                        ◇AQ54
                        ♣AK1084
    ♠109873                         ♠K42
    ♡A10965        ┌─────────┐      ♡872
    ◇8             │    N    │      ◇109732
    ♣95            │  W   E  │      ♣Q6
                   │    S    │
                   └─────────┘
                        ♠AQJ6
                        ♡K4
                        ◇KJ6
                        ♣J732
```

This was the Spanish bidding:

| West | North | East | South |
|------|-------|------|-------|
| Pass | 1♣ | Pass | 1♠ |
| Pass | 2◇ | Pass | 4♣ |
| Pass | 4NT | Pass | 5◇ |
| Pass | 6♣ | All Pass | |

A fair sequence, and the slam was made when the trumps broke. "I would have liked to play in 6NT," remarked South, "but you bid no-trumps first."

At the other table North at some point bid four spades to show his control and South became declarer in 6NT. He won the spade lead and had time to do a little fishing around before deciding how to play the clubs. When he found West with a singleton diamond it seemed reasonable to place him with the longer clubs, so the declarer, having previously cashed the ace of clubs, decided to finesse on the next round. Any moral? No, I think it was just one of those things.

# Denmark v. Spain

The Danes played cleverly at one table, luckily at the other; it amounted to a big swing.

*East-West game; Dealer South.*

```
                    ♠ K 8 5 4
                    ♡ A 9 4
                    ♢ 9 8 7 6
                    ♣ Q J
    ♠ 10 7 3 2            N            ♠ J
    ♡ K 2           W         E        ♡ Q J 10 6 3
    ♢ A 10               S            ♢ K
    ♣ 9 8 5 4 3                        ♣ A K 10 7 6 2
                    ♠ A Q 9 6
                    ♡ 8 7 5
                    ♢ Q J 5 4 3 2
                    ♣ None
```

**Open room**

| West | North | East | South |
|------|-------|------|-------|
| | Adamsen | | Nicolaisen |
| | | | 1♠ |
| Pass | 2♠ | 3♡ | Pass |
| 4♡ | All Pass | | |

South's one spade opening was in accordance with the system — a biddable suit and 8–11 points.

And South led — the six of spades! North was happy to play the king (South could hardly have led low from QJ9x), and a club back, followed by a heart to the ace and another ruff, led to a penalty of 100.

**Closed room**

| West | North | East | South |
|------|-------|------|-------|
| Grauland | | Christiansen | |
| | | | Pass |
| Pass | Pass | 1♣ | 1♢ |
| 2♣ | 2♢ | 2♡ | 4♢ |
| 5♣ | 5♢ | 5♡ | Pass |
| 6♣ | Pass | Pass | Double |
| All Pass | | | |

Would it be one down, 200 against 100, three points to Spain, or would he make it, for 1540 and 17 points to Denmark? South led the queen of diamonds, so it was 17 to Denmark.

# Standings after Round 12 (Day Six)

| | | | | | |
|---|---|---:|---|---|---:|
| 1. | Iceland | 235 | 14. | Germany | 180 |
| 2. | Sweden | 232 | 15. | Turkey | 177 |
| 3. | Great Britain | 228.5 | 16. | Austria | 176 |
| 4. | Poland | 225 | 17. | Czechoslovakia | 170 |
| 5. | Norway | 214 | 18. | Portugal | 169 |
| 6. | USSR | 210 | 19. | Ireland | 165.5 |
| 7. | Netherlands | 200 | 20. | Greece | 163 |
| 8. | Hungary | 199 | 21. | Belgium | 156 |
| 9. | France | 193 | 22. | Bulgaria | 150 |
| 10. | Israel | 192.5 | 23. | Switzerland | 133 |
| 11. | Finland | 191 | 24. | Liechtenstein | 131.5 |
| 12. | Italy | 185 | 25. | Spain | 116 |
| 13. | Denmark | 183 | 26. | Yugoslavia | 87 |

I seem to have been wrong about Iceland, who have stayed at the top, right about the Netherlands, who are climbing fast. The French expert, Pierre Schemeil, points out that his team had a difficult draw and will soon be near the top.

The leading scores in the Ladies Teams after six rounds are: Israel 129, Germany 118, Austria 117.5, Britain 113.5, France 109, Italy 102.5, Denmark 101. Still everything to play for in both events.

# Day Seven

## Poland v. USSR

*The Polish Team.*

This match attracted much interest and resulted in a 15–15 draw, despite the fact that the Russians lost a lot of points on the two hands I describe. This was the first:

*Game all; Dealer South.*

```
              ♠ 10 7 5 3
              ♡ K 10 7 6 5 4 3
              ◇ 5
              ♣ Q
♠ A Q 4 2          N          ♠ J 6
♡ 9           W       E       ♡ J 2
◇ J 10 9 4 2               ◇ A K 7
♣ A J 3           S          ♣ K 10 9 6 5 4
              ♠ K 9 8
              ♡ A Q 8
              ◇ Q 8 6 3
              ♣ 8 7 2
```

Here the Russians played in five clubs. North-South had bid hearts at some point and Spiridonov, South, began with the ace of hearts. What do you suppose he played next, and why?

He might have tried a spade, or even a club, but instead he played a second heart. The declarer thought this might well be to prevent him from playing king and another club, so he came to hand and finessed the jack of clubs. Unlucky, one down, as there was no way of avoiding a diamond loser.

On the second occasion I think one must blame the Russian declarer.

*North-South game; Dealer West.*

```
                  ♠9532
                  ♡8
                  ◇K43
                  ♣J10962
  ♠KJ874        ┌──────┐        ♠None
  ♡QJ107        │   N  │        ♡AK54
  ◇1082         │ W  E │        ◇AQJ7
  ♣7            │   S  │        ♣AKQ53
                └──────┘
                  ♠AQ106
                  ♡9632
                  ◇965
                  ♣84
```

When Poland was East-West, South led a diamond against six hearts, which was made. The Russian West was declarer in seven hearts and now North led a low diamond. Experience tells that one must take the finesse on these occasions; the play is going to be too difficult if you go up with the ace, discard two diamonds on the clubs, and so forth. After a diamond has run to the ten declarer must play on the dummy taking two club ruffs in hand.

# Britain v. Ireland (ladies)

This traditional encounter attracted the biggest audience yet in the Bridgerama hall; fortunately, there was none of the usual English insistence that no one should sit on the gangways lest the whole building burst into flames.

The match was even thoughout, so that all depended on the final board.

*East-West game; Dealer West.*

```
                  ♠ K 10 8 4 2
                  ♡ A 8 4
                  ◇ 2
                  ♣ A Q 6 2
  ♠ 9 6 5                          ♠ A Q 3
  ♡ Q            ┌─────────┐       ♡ J 10 9 6 2
  ◇ K 9 8 6 4    │ W  N  E │       ◇ J 7 5 3
  ♣ 10 9 8 5     │    S    │       ♣ 4
                 └─────────┘
                  ♠ J 7
                  ♡ K 7 5 3
                  ◇ A Q 10
                  ♣ K J 7 3
```

The Irish North opened one spade and South, Rebecca O'Keefe, playing with her mother, responded 3NT, an absolutely splendid call of a type I have made in every form of the game for fifty years; now, alas, a despised and dying breed. However, her play was not so bright. West led a diamond to the jack and queen and South's first move was one round of clubs, followed by two rounds of hearts. After this, there wasn't much hope as the cards lay.

At the other table the beginning in 3NT was the same, but after winning the first diamond Sandra Penfold played four rounds of clubs, finishing in dummy. As Patrick Jourdain modestly reminded us, this was the essence of his Bols Tip some years ago: *In 3NT, with eight winners, cash your long suit.*

This sequence of play was embarrassing for East. She could discard a heart and a spade without too much pain, but what then? The only possibility was a diamond, but then a low spade from the table (good play in itself) was followed by the ten from hand on the next diamond; from now on, West was out of the game and South was able to set up her ninth trick in spades.

# Day Eight

## Britain v. Belgium

Rixi Markus arrived yesterday and when I asked her if she had seen any interesting hands she produced four or five in quick time. Here she disapproved of South's lead and also of the declarer's play.

*Game all; Dealer North.*

```
              ♠ J 8 4
              ♡ A 9 8 5 4 3
              ◇ Q
              ♣ Q 10 7
  ♠ A 9 7              N        ♠ K Q 10 6 2
  ♡ K Q J        W        E     ♡ None
  ◇ 10 4 3 2           S        ◇ K J 9 8 6
  ♣ J 6 4                       ♣ A K 9
              ♠ 5 3
              ♡ 10 7 6 2
              ◇ A 7 5
              ♣ 8 5 3 2
```

With Britain North-South the bidding went:

| West | North | East | South |
|------|-------|------|-------|
|      | Pass  | 1 ♠  | Pass  |
| 2 ♠  | 3 ♡   | 6 ♠  | All Pass |

Not many players would have bid simply two spades on the West hand (11 points!) but I like it.

Forrester led a low heart. "How can he do that?" Rixi demanded. "Obviously East is expecting a heart lead. I would have led the ace of diamonds."

Declarer ruffed the heart and then did a funny thing: he played a low spade to the nine, which was not a success; in fact it meant two down.

What induced the declarer to play South for J x x x in trumps? I suppose he thought that North had risked three hearts because he had a singleton spade; but it was just as likely that he held three or four spades and expected his partner to be short. Or perhaps declarer was taking an unusual view of the hand because his side was a lot down at half time.

# Norway v. Turkey

Norwegian players have always been proud of their slam bidding, sometimes on exiguous values. The editor of their magazine, Tommy Sandsmark, told me of two from this tournament. The first was bid and played by one of their debutantes, Helge Hantveit.

*North-South game; Dealer South.*

```
              ♠A943
              ♡AK9
              ◇82
              ♣J543
♠10                        ♠J87
♡Q10876        N           ♡J3
◇QJ943     W     E         ◇105
♣Q9            S           ♣A108762
              ♠KQ652
              ♡542
              ◇AK76
              ♣K
```

| West | North | East | South |
|------|-------|------|-------|
| Zorlu | Thomassen | Kubak | Hantveit |
| | | | 1♠ |
| Pass | 1NT | Pass | 2◇ |
| Pass | 2NT | Pass | 3♡ |
| Pass | 4NT | Pass | 5◇ |
| Pass | 6♠ | All Pass | |

Both 1NT and 2NT were relays. Only 27 points in the two hands, including a singleton king, which nevertheless pulled its weight.

Since the opponents seemed to have strength in the other three suits, West began with the quaint lead of a low club. East won and switched to a spade. On the next spade West discarded a heart. A club ruff brought down the queen, and East's 3–6 distribution was revealed. Now came a heart to the ace and a club ruff, king of spades, a heart to the king and the jack of clubs, leaving:

```
              ♠ 9
              ♡ 9
              ◇ 8 2
              ♣ None
♠ None        ┌─────────┐
♡ Q           │    N    │
◇ Q J 9       │ W     E │        immaterial
♣ None        │    S    │
              └─────────┘
              ♠ None
              ♡ 2
              ◇ A K 7
              ♣ None
```

Now the nine of spades, squeezing West, an ending impossible to visualise at the beginning of the play.

*Tommy Sandsmark of Norway.*

# Norway v. Sweden

This was the second of the Norwegian slams (see previous deal).

*Game all; Dealer South.*

```
                    ♠ A J 2
                    ♡ A 3
                    ◇ A Q 10 8 5
                    ♣ A 5 3
   ♠ 9 7 5 4 3                        ♠ 10 8
   ♡ Q 8 5 4         N               ♡ J 10 9 6
   ◇ 2           W       E           ◇ J 6 3
   ♣ K J 7           S               ♣ 10 8 6 2
                    ♠ K Q 6
                    ♡ K 7 2
                    ◇ K 9 7 4
                    ♣ Q 9 4
```

| West | North | East | South |
|------|-------|------|-------|
|      | *Thomassen* |  | *Hantveit* |
|      |       |      | 1 NT |
| Pass | 2 ♣ | Pass | 2 ◇ |
| Pass | 6 NT | All Pass |  |

You would rather be in six diamonds, although this does not necessarily provide more tricks, because the only ruff has to be taken in the long trump hand.

West led a spade, which went to the king. After three spades and four diamonds the position was:

```
                    ♠ None
                    ♡ A 3
                    ◇ 5
                    ♣ A 5 3
   ♠ None                             ♠ None
   ♡ Q 8 5          N                ♡ J 10 9
   ◇ None       W       E            ◇ None
   ♣ K J 7          S                ♣ 10 8 6
                    ♠ None
                    ♡ K 7 2
                    ◇ None
                    ♣ Q 9 4
```

Now came the last diamond and East-West were in a bad way. If East throws a heart, South throws a club and West can be end-played. If East discards a club on the fifth diamond South discards a heart, and so must West; then a low club to the nine wins the contract.

Of course, there is a double-dummy element in the end-play, and at the other table the Swedish declarer did not place the cards so well. In the match between Britain and Czechoslovakia the British, in six diamonds, eliminated and played a club to the nine. I was given a learned exposition of why this was done, but I must say I didn't quite follow the argument. The Czechs at the other table misread the end position.

———————————

A small dispute is in progress because the German ladies are reluctant to play on Rama. Earlier on, we are told, they played a little joke on their Austrian neighbours, adopting new name badges, such as Mrs C. Atastrophy. At last one of the Austrian ladies said to an opponent, "Why, dear, I didn't know you'd been married recently."

*The German ladies' team.*

# Denmark v. Austria (ladies)

*Austrian Gabi Bamberger chooses the right card.*

If the Austrian ladies, who are in the lead at the moment, win the championship they may be glad to have survived the following deal, which everywhere else was 420 to East-West. North-South were the fine Danish pair, Kirsten Steen Møller–Judy Norris.

*Love all; Dealer North.*

```
                    ♠ 10 5
                    ♡ Q 8 7
                    ◇ A 6 4 3
                    ♣ K 8 7 2
    ♠ A K 6 4         ┌─────────┐        ♠ 9 7
    ♡ 10 9 3 2        │   N     │        ♡ K J 6 5 4
    ◇ Q 10 2         │ W   E   │        ◇ K J
    ♣ 6 3            │   S     │        ♣ A Q 10 9
                     └─────────┘
                    ♠ Q J 8 3 2
                    ♡ A
                    ◇ 9 8 7 5
                    ♣ J 5 4
```

With the Austrians East-West, the bidding went:

| West | North | East | South |
|------|-------|------|-------|
|      | Pass  | 1♡   | Pass  |
| 3♡   | Pass  | 4♡   | All Pass |

In four hearts, after a spade lead, you are going to lose a heart and a diamond, presumably; but if you take your eye off the ball . . .

The declarer won with the king of spades and (foolishly) set about establishing an extra diamond by leading a diamond to the king and overtaking the jack. North won and returned her second spade to the ace. East took a club discard on the ten of diamonds, then ran the ten of hearts to South's ace. South played a third spade, on which North discarded a club while the declarer ruffed. She was now at this point:

```
              ♠ None
              ♡ Q 8
              ◇ 6
              ♣ K 8 7
♠ 6                           ♠ None
♡ 9 3 2         N             ♡ K J 6
◇ None      W     E           ◇ None
♣ 6 3          S              ♣ A Q 10
              ♠ 8 3
              ♡ None
              ◇ 9
              ♣ J 5 4
```

Where have all those lovely entries gone to? East exited with ace and ten of clubs (ace and queen would have been better as the cards lay, because North was likely to hold the king). Now the eight of spades, on which North's last club was thrown; so the queen of hearts became a fourth winner for the defence.

## Modern bidding

Turning for a few moments from serious analysis, here is a deal from the 14th round of the Open series which gave rise to at least one 'unusual' sequence; except, alas, that such sequences are not unusual at all.

*East-West game; Dealer South.*

```
              ♠ A
              ♡ 5 4
              ♢ J 8 4 2
              ♣ A K Q J 8 6
  ♠ 10 9 8 5 3        N        ♠ Q J 7
  ♡ 9 8 6 3      W       E     ♡ 10 7
  ♢ Q 6 3            S         ♢ 9 7 5
  ♣ 2                          ♣ 10 7 5 4 3
              ♠ K 6 4 2
              ♡ A K Q J 2
              ♢ A K 10
              ♣ 9
```

This was one sequence, proposed (with tongue in cheek) by a correspondent named Robert Schorling as an entry for the best bid hand of the tournament:

| South | North |
|-------|-------|
| Pass  | 2♡    |
| 2♠    | 3♡    |
| 3♠    | 4♡    |
| 4♠    | 4NT   |
| 5NT   | 6♢    |
| 7NT   | Pass  |

He made it all right (seven clubs fails, as you see), but he wouldn't have made it against me. I would have left the building.

That highly conventional bidding is not *always* succcessful was demonstrated on a hand, not worth setting out in detail, where East-West held every ace and king except in diamonds, where the holding was KQxxx opposite J1098xxx. To show that I am not making it up, seven diamonds was bid by Bulgaria, Ireland, Liechtenstein, Czechoslovakia, and *both* tables of Britain v. Greece. Finally, the Poles managed (but didn't make) 7NT!

### A two-way double

Who wants to be a tournament director? Claude Dadoun was called to a table in a Ladies match where the bidding had begun:

| West | North | East | South |
|------|-------|------|-------|
|      | 3 ♠   | Double | Director! |

South: "I asked West about the meaning of the double, and this was her reply: 'If three spades is natural the double is for take-out, and if it's a pre-empt in a minor the double is for penalties.'"

*Doris Fischer, a member of the victorious Austrian ladies' team.*

# Day Nine

## Britain v. Russia

The Russians had done extremely well so far, always in the top third, but I must say it was difficult to see why on the evidence of this match. The British played poorly too. This was an early board:

*East-West game; Dealer South.*

```
                    ♠2
                    ♡Q4
                    ◇AK1074
                    ♣K10976
    ♠AJ74          ┌─────┐        ♠Q86
    ♡K9853         │  N  │        ♡A1076
    ◇QJ            │W   E│        ◇93
    ♣J2            │  S  │        ♣AQ43
                   └─────┘
                    ♠K10953
                    ♡J2
                    ◇8652
                    ♣85
```

Nothing much happened in the closed room. Armstrong, West, opened one heart and North overcalled with 2NT — the world's most overplayed convention. East raised to four hearts and West made ten tricks, 620.

The audience in the open room had more excitement.

| West | North | East | South |
|------|-------|------|-------|
| *Spiridinov* | *Robson* | *Baguzin* | *Forrester* |
| | | | 2◇ |
| 2♡ | 2NT | 4♡ | Pass |
| Pass | Double | Redouble | 4♠ |
| Double | 4NT | Pass | 5◇ |
| Pass | Pass | Double | All Pass |

Forrester's two diamond opening showed in theory a major-minor two-suiter in the 5-9 range. He can hardly have been happy to finish in five diamonds doubled.

"The defence can cash two hearts, a spade, two clubs, and a club overruff," opined the commentators. But it didn't go quite like that. West led the jack of diamonds, dummy won, and a spade went to the ten and jack. The defenders took their two heart tricks, and then West led the jack of clubs.

"This is going to be murder," declared Ron Andersen from the bench. "Two clubs and a ruff, 800." Missing one or two points in the play, perhaps, Baguzin headed the club king with the ace, returned a trump, and then (having failed to revise his count of the hand) allowed South to sneak a trick with a low club to the eight. That was only two down and 8 IMPs to Britain.

*The Commentary team: Dirk Schroeder, Greer Mackenzie, Ron Andersen in full cry and Barry Rigal.*

# Britain v. Russia

The hands in this match were not dramatic, but some were instructive, such as:

*East-West game; Dealer North.*

```
              ♠ K 5 3 2
              ♡ K Q J 9
              ◇ Q
              ♣ 9 7 6 3
♠ A J 10 9 7 4    ┌─────┐      ♠ Q 8
♡ 4 2             │  N  │      ♡ 10 8 5 3
◇ J 4            │ W E │      ◇ K 10 9 7
♣ A 10 2         │  S  │      ♣ K Q 4
                 └─────┘
              ♠ 6
              ♡ A 7 6
              ◇ A 8 6 5 3 2
              ♣ J 8 5
```

This was the sequence when Robson and Forrester were North-South:

| West | North | East | South |
|------|-------|------|-------|
| | *Robson* | | *Forrester* |
| | Pass | Pass | 1◇ |
| 1♠ | Double | Pass [1] | 2◇ |
| 2♠ | Pass | Pass | 3♣ [2] |
| Pass | Pass | 3NT [3] | Pass |
| Pass | Double | All Pass | |

[1] So silly to pass at this point instead of giving a picture of the fair values by bidding 1NT.

[2] A bit mysterious; perhaps, in their methods, he had to give partner another chance, or maybe he feared (reasonably enough) that two spades would be good for the opposition.

[3] This is really awful, with no aces and the opponents marked with fair values.

Forrester led a low heart (the suit where his partner was sure to hold values) and the defenders took six tricks, for 500.

At the other table the British East-West were one down in three spades and may have been surprised to find that the team had picked up nine match points. Britain won the match 21–9.

From:
**George Perry**

T22/138
ext. 2518

Another hand that made me wonder about the Russian bidding was when West and East held:

♠986432               ♠AKJ
♡4                      ♡AJ32
◇AQJ10            ◇84
♣K7                ♣10932

```
        N
     W     E
        S
```

At game all West passed in second hand (it *must* be right to open one spade), North opened one heart, South responded two hearts, and now West came in with two spades. East *passed* without a moment's thought; five was cold.

*Raymond Brock, Chairman of the BBL, collects the Generali trophy on behalf of Britain, the most successful nation in Europe in 1991.*

# France v. Yugoslavia

I remarked early on that the young French player, Jean-Christophe Quantin, was likely to be one of the stars of the tournament, but as things have turned out the French players have not been in the limelight. Here, however, is a very pretty defence that he and Abécassis played against Yugoslavia.

*Game all; Dealer West.*

```
              ♠ A Q 10 5 2
              ♡ K 10 2
              ◇ 3
              ♣ K Q 9 7
  ♠ K J 9 4        N         ♠ 8
  ♡ J 5 2     W       E      ♡ 9 8 7 6 3
  ◇ K 9 2         S          ◇ A 7 6
  ♣ 6 4 2                    ♣ A 8 5 3
              ♠ 7 6 3
              ♡ A Q
              ◇ Q J 10 8 5 4
              ♣ J 10
```

| West | North | East | South |
|------|-------|------|-------|
| *Abécassis* | | *Quantin* | |
| Pass | 1♠ | Pass | 1 NT |
| Pass | 2♣ | Pass | 3♠ |
| Pass | 4♠ | All Pass | |

East led a heart, won in dummy, and South played a spade to the *ace*, perhaps thinking that this was a safety play. (Two finesses is the best play for four tricks with this combination.) He then crossed to the ace of hearts and led a second spade, on which West played low and the ten won. He followed with a small club; Quantin went up with the ace and led a *low* diamond. It was, of course, clear that the declarer did not hold the diamond king.

Abécassis won with the king and returned a diamond, which North had to ruff. A club to the jack was followed by a spade. Now West, who still had the king and jack of spades, went up with the king and played a third diamond, which forced the declarer's last trump. The defenders made two aces and two trump tricks.

A correspondent who signs herself with the initials T.K.K. has contributed several amusing pieces to the Bulletin. She has now identified three relatively unknown players, namely:

The Pope's niece:    Bundelli (Italy)
Dutch champion:    Elly Unbidtail
English dragon:    I.I. Landybullet

Get it? The names are all anagrams of Daily Bulletin.

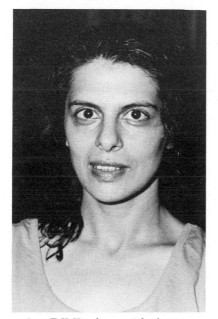

*The mysterious T.K.K. whose articles became an essential part of the Killarney bulletin.*

# Finland v. Turkey

When the deal below was played on Rama between Britain and Russia both sides played in three spades, just made, and the commentators noted simply that four hearts by East-West would have had chances. In fact, this was the contract at five of the 24 tables. The play between Finland and Turkey was rightly described by Barry Rigal as perhaps the defence of the tournament.

*Game all; Dealer West.*

```
              ♠ Q 10 6
              ♡ Q
              ◇ J 6 2
              ♣ Q J 9 7 3 2
  ♠ K 8 5          N          ♠ 7 3
  ♡ K 7 6 5 3 2  W   E        ♡ A J 9 8
  ◇ A 7 3          S          ◇ Q 9 8 5
  ♣ K                         ♣ 8 6 4
              ♠ A J 9 4 2
              ♡ 10 4
              ◇ K 10 4
              ♣ A 10 5
```

| West | North | East | South |
|------|-------|------|-------|
| *Vihtila* | *Zorlu* | *Jouni* | *Kubac* |
| 1 ♡ | Pass | 2 ♡ | 2 ♠ |
| 3 ◇ | 3 ♠ | 4 ♡ | All Pass |

The play went as you would expect: club to ace, ace and another spade; trumps were drawn and the losers in spades and clubs were eliminated, leading to this ending, with West to play:

```
              ♠ None
              ♡ None
              ◇ J 6 2
              ♣ J 9
  ♠ None           N          ♠ None
  ♡ 7 6        W   E          ♡ 9
  ◇ A 7 3          S          ◇ Q 9 8 5
  ♣ None                      ♣ None
              ♠ J 9
              ♡ None
              ◇ K 10 4
              ♣ None
```

The declarer led a low diamond. Everyone knows the position that may arise when dummy's diamonds are Qxxx: then it is important for North to insert the jack, protecting South from an end-play when his diamonds are such as K109.

The play seems pointless when you can see Q98x on the table. But of course it's not, and Zorlu saw this. When the jack of diamonds was played the declarer had to judge whether North had played this card from Jxx or J10x, in which case it would be right to duck in dummy. Not surprisingly, he guessed wrong.

# Norway v. Netherlands

Used there not to be an aphorism along the lines of 'take care of the pence and the pounds will take care of themselves'? The Norwegian declarer might have thought of that when playing the deal below in six hearts.

*East-West game; Dealer West.*

```
              ♠ A 10 7 2
              ♡ J 9 8 6 4
              ◇ 8
              ♣ K J 6
♠ 9 8 5 4         N         ♠ K Q J 6
♡ None      W         E     ♡ 10 7 3
◇ A K 5 3 2       S         ◇ Q 10 9 6
♣ Q 9 8 2                   ♣ 5 3
              ♠ 3
              ♡ A K Q 5 2
              ◇ J 7 4
              ♣ A 10 7 4
```

Glen Groetheim, Norway, (we don't hide names in this book), bid well to reach six hearts on the North-South cards. West began with the ace of diamonds and switched to a spade. The declarer won, ruffed a spade high, and led the two of hearts to the jack, discovering West's void. Now, I can assure you, it is impossible to arrive at twelve tricks even though you play West for the queen of clubs.

Suppose that instead of leading that low heart to the jack you play the two top hearts from hand. That leaves:

```
              ♠ 10 7
              ♡ J 9 8
              ◇ None
              ♣ K J 6
♠ 9 8            N          ♠ K Q
♡ None      W         E     ♡ 10
◇ K 5             S         ◇ Q 10 6
♣ Q 9 8 2                   ♣ 5 3
              ♠ None
              ♡ 5 2
              ◇ J 7
              ♣ A 10 7 4
```

Now ruff a diamond, ruff a spade, ruff a diamond, ruff a

spade. You will still need to find the queen of clubs, but that won't be difficult, particularly as West had made a second-round double of the one heart opening.

The Netherlands won what Barry Rigal called 'A disappointing match' by 25–3. Disappointing for some, anyway.

## Standings after Round 18 (Day Nine)

| | | | | |
|---|---|---|---|---|
| 1. | Great Britain | 362.5 | 14. Finland | 265 |
| 2. | Sweden | 356 | 14. Austria | 265 |
| 3. | Iceland | 346 | 16. Turkey | 261 |
| 4. | Poland | 334 | 17. Belgium | 255 |
| 5. | Netherlands | 326 | 18. Greece | 229 |
| 6. | France | 324 | 19. Ireland | 227.5 |
| 7. | Norway | 308 | 20. Bulgaria | 223 |
| 8. | USSR | 307 | 21. Czechoslovakia | 221 |
| 9. | Italy | 298 | 22. Portugal | 220 |
| 10. | Denmark | 289 | 23. Liechtenstein | 205.5 |
| 11. | Hungary | 288 | 24. Switzerland | 201 |
| 12. | Israel | 287.5 | 25. Spain | 195 |
| 13. | Germany | 268 | 26. Yugoslavia | 157 |

Tomorrow's match between Britain and Sweden is obviously going to be important, and perhaps decisive. On the whole, one must say that this tournament is going very much according to form and expectation.

## Ladies Teams (after 10 rounds)

| | | | | |
|---|---|---|---|---|
| 1. | Austria | 208.5 | 10. Ireland | 151 |
| 2. | Denmark | 188 | 11. Poland | 130 |
| 3. | Great Britain | 186.5 | 12. Turkey | 120 |
| 4. | Germany | 186 | 13. Spain | 118.5 |
| 5. | Netherlands | 183 | 14. Belgium | 108.5 |
| 6. | France | 172 | 15. San Marino | 101 |
| 7. | Israel | 171 | 16. USSR | 97.5 |
| 8. | Italy | 162 | 17. Finland | 86.5 |
| 9. | Sweden | 159 | | |

Israel fell back sharply after taking the early lead. Did I fail to mention Austria as one of the favourites? Oh well, there was a time when Austria was not so well fancied. The British team is playing well, according to its captain, Chris Dixon. Tomorrow's match against Denmark will be critical.

# Day Ten

## Britain v. Sweden

These were the top teams, with the nearest rivals 20 points away, so a big win for either side was almost sure to be decisive. The match began rather unsatisfactorily, with an appeal on board one. The tournament director's ruling was for the most part in Britain's favour, but it seems a further appeal may follow. All scores are subject to the determination of this affair.

On an early board a point arose that will be familiar to experienced players. West and East hold:

```
♠A7              N              ♠KJ1092
♡Q10          W     E           ♡3
♢A10983          S              ♢KJ74
♣Q832                           ♣A107
```

East is in four spades, after North has overcalled one heart. South leads a heart to North's king and declarer ruffs the heart continuation. What should he do next?

The best line to avoid losing control of the trumps is to run the jack of spades. If it loses, at least you cannot be forced again in hearts. The full hand was:

*East-West game; Dealer South.*

```
                 ♠543
                 ♡AK854
                 ♢65
                 ♣K54
♠A7              N              ♠KJ1092
♡Q10          W     E           ♡3
♢A10983          S              ♢KJ74
♣Q832                           ♣A107
                 ♠Q86
                 ♡J9762
                 ♢Q2
                 ♣J96
```

Kirby ran the jack of spades, as suggested, and when it held, and the main suits broke well, he made an overtrick.

Nilsland, at the other table, crossed to the ace of diamonds at trick three, presumably because he thought North was more likely to hold the spade queen. When the finesse lost he was in some discomfort, but he managed to make ten tricks in the end.

*The Swedish team are happy with their score in this important match.*

## Modern world

On board 23 of Israel v. Poland three players bid diamonds. One player held ♢AKQ954. He was the one who did not bid diamonds.

# Britain v. Sweden

The Swedes had a fair early lead, but the British pulled them back and to my mind looked the better team. When Robson picked up the North cards on the following deal he may have looked forward to a small respite from his labours, but it wasn't so.

*North-South game; Dealer East.*

```
                    ♠ 109643
                    ♡ 763
                    ◇ 7
                    ♣ 8642
        ♠ Q872        ┌─────┐      ♠ KJ5
        ♡ KQ102       │  N  │      ♡ 984
        ◇ A84         │ W E │      ◇ KQ105
        ♣ A7          │  S  │      ♣ Q53
                      └─────┘
                    ♠ A
                    ♡ AJ5
                    ◇ J9632
                    ♣ KJ109
```

| West | North | East | South |
|------|-------|------|-------|
|      | Robson |     | Forrester |
|      |       | 1♣ | 1NT |
| Double | 2♣ | Double | All Pass |

Pretty keen stuff. East opens one club on a poor hand and has the hardihood to double two clubs on the next round. South's 1NT, of course, showed values in the minors.

When two clubs doubled was passed out, East made the standard lead in these situations — a trump. After his usual careful thought Robson played the *king* from dummy. Cheers, and a few jeers, from the Swedish supporters, puzzled head-shaking by the British. The sequel was horrible. Three rounds of trumps held North to two aces and three trumps, 800 for three down.

There was a general belief among the spectators that the declarer had committed an outstanding folly by going up with the king of clubs instead of putting in the ten. But think: if East has led from Axx, which if anything is more likely than Qxx, then the king will hold and when the defenders win the first diamond their trumps will be blocked. It will be best now for East to overtake the queen of trumps and play a third round, but he may not realise this so early in the play.

*The Swedish Open team that finished runners-up.*

# Britain v. Sweden

The deal below looks innocent and easy, but when you are playing against a 'funny' system few hands are straightforward.

*Love all; Dealer West.*

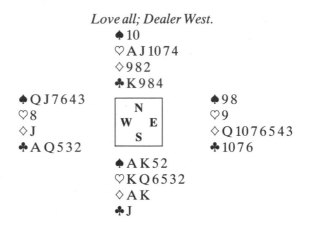

```
              ♠ 10
              ♡ A J 10 7 4
              ◇ 9 8 2
              ♣ K 9 8 4
♠ Q J 7 6 4 3              ♠ 9 8
♡ 8            N          ♡ 9
◇ J        W     E        ◇ Q 10 7 6 5 4 3
♣ A Q 5 3 2    S          ♣ 10 7 6
              ♠ A K 5 2
              ♡ K Q 6 5 3 2
              ◇ A K
              ♣ J
```

West opened one spade and his side made two more calls, but the Swedish pair soon reached the slam.

| West | North | East | South |
|---|---|---|---|
| *Armstrong* | *Gullberg* | *Kirby* | *Sundelin* |
| 1♠ | Pass | 1 NT | Double |
| 2♣ | 3♡ | Pass | 4 NT |
| Pass | 5◇ | Pass | 6♡ |
| All Pass | | | |

This was the sequence in the open room:

| West | North | East | South |
|---|---|---|---|
| *Fallenius* | *Robson* | *Nilsland* | *Forrester* |
| 2◇ | Pass | 2♡ | Pass |
| 3♠ | Pass | Pass | 4♡ |
| All Pass | | | |

West's two diamonds showed two suits of the same colour and South passed two hearts because double would be for take-out. West's three spades, showing upper range of his type, proved awkward for South, who had no chance now to indicate his great strength. Robson looked at his hand for a while but could hardly bid on.

It seems to me that to pass such a big hand as South held is tactically wrong. (Tell Boris Schapiro to do that and see what answer you get!) It is going to be very difficult to give a picture later. If he doubles now he may be able to show his true colours on the next round after West has shown the black suits.

Sweden won 16–14.

---

### It follows

Marcel Winkel, in the Pressroom, answered the phone and the conversation went: Caller: "My name is Quinn." Marcel: "Double N?" Caller: "Yes, from Dublin."

*Roman Smolski.*

# Denmark v. Italy (ladies)

Most players have an understanding that a surprise double after 1NT–3NT contains a special message. It means that the doubler has a strong suit and is desperately keen that his partner should find the right lead. The double is usually made when the defender has a suit such as A K Q x x x, or possibly K Q J 10 x and a side ace.

In a ladies match between Denmark and Italy the Italian pair, Bilde–Gilleborg, made a double of this sort. It was a big success. The question that was put to me was: which of the Danish players should have run?

*East-West game; Dealer South.*

```
                ♠ 7 6
                ♡ 6 5
                ◇ Q 5
                ♣ A K J 10 9 7 6
   ♠ 1042          N          ♠ A K Q 9 8 5
   ♡ J 9 4 3 2   W   E        ♡ Q 8 7
   ◇ K 6 3          S         ◇ 10 8 7 2
   ♣ 5 4                      ♣ None
                ♠ J 3
                ♡ A K 10
                ◇ A J 9 4
                ♣ Q 8 3 2
```

| West | North | East | South |
|------|-------|------|-------|
|      |       |      | 1 NT  |
| Pass | 3 NT  | Double | All Pass |

West led his shorter major — normal in these situations — and North-South yielded 300,

Most people would say that North should run, because he has the long suit and three unguarded suits. However, there is something to be said on the other side. South can be fairly sure that the double is for a spade, so perhaps he is the one who should take out into four clubs.

---

I heard the captain of one of the ladies' teams — I think it was Spain — complaining that his players were not strong on safety plays.

"There are one or two good books," I began...

"I know all about that," he interrupted, "but I don't remember your mentioning this one. My girl was in three hearts, with three side losers, and in trumps she had a singleton opposite A Q J 8 7 6 4. She finessed and lost to a singleton king."

That's right. If the defender under the long suit has four trumps to the king you must lose two tricks whatever you do.

# Sweden v. Israel

Israel has its ups and downs in the European championship, perhaps because some of its best players move to other pastures. Sweden is always strong. The first big swing occurred on this deal:

*Love all; Dealer West.*

```
              ♠ A J 8 3
              ♡ 8
              ◇ K 9 6
              ♣ K Q 9 7 4
♠ Q 10 9 4 2        ┌─────────┐        ♠ K 7
♡ A 6              │    N    │        ♡ K 10 9 7 5
◇ A 8 7           │ W     E │        ◇ Q J 10 4 3
♣ J 6 3           │    S    │        ♣ 10
                   └─────────┘
              ♠ 6 5
              ♡ Q J 4 3 2
              ◇ 5 2
              ♣ A 8 5 2
```

**Closed room**

| West | North | East | South |
|------|-------|------|-------|
| *Aviram* | *Morath* | *Porat* | *Bierregard* |
| Pass | 1♣ | 2♡ | Pass |
| 2 NT | Pass | 3◇ | Pass |
| 3♡ | Pass | Pass | Double |
| All Pass | | | |

If it is admitted that East's two heart overcall was dangerous, one may ask, what should he bid? "It looks a normal Michaels cue-bid (i.e. two spades) to your reporter," declared Patrick Jourdain in the Bulletin. If you are playing for Welsh leeks, possibly. I think these overcalls are ridiculously overdone. Pass and see what happens.

A technical point: on the sequence that occurred, can West pass three diamonds? I don't see why not, though no one ever does. The declarer made heavy weather of the play and went three down.

**Open room**

| West | North | East | South |
|------|-------|------|-------|
| *Sundelin* | *Altshuler* | *Gullberg* | *Kaufman* |
| 1♠ | 2♣ | Double | 3♣ |
| 3♠ | All Pass | | |

Playing with what Patrick called 'lengthy tenacity', Sundelin was one down in this contract. This was 10 IMPs to the Swedes, who won the match 20–10.

*The organisers face the press barrage: Panos Gerontopoulos, José Damiani (President of the European Bridge League), Ernesto D'Orsi (President of the World Bridge Federation) and Tommy Sandsmark.*

# Britain v. Greece

The Greeks started this tournament very well — I think they held the lead early on. Since then they have had a number of poor results, but for a while their match against Britain was keenly contested.

*North-South game; Dealer East.*

```
              ♠ K 5 4 2
              ♡ Q 5 3
              ◇ K 10 7 4
              ♣ 7 2
  ♠ Q 9 6                      ♠ A J 8 7 3
  ♡ J 9 2        N             ♡ A 7 6 4
  ◇ Q 8 5     W     E          ◇ None
  ♣ A J 10 4     S             ♣ 9 8 6 3
              ♠ 10
              ♡ K 10 8
              ◇ A J 9 6 3 2
              ♣ K Q 5
```

Forrester and Robson may make the game difficult for their opponents, but they don't make it particularly easy for one another. See if you can keep track of this auction:

| West | North | East | South |
|------|-------|------|-------|
| *Forrester* | | *Robson* | |
| | | Pass | 1 ◇ |
| Pass | 1 ♠ | Pass | 2 ◇ |
| Pass | Pass | Double | Pass |
| 2 ♡ | 3 ◇ | Double [1] | Pass |
| 4 ♣ | Pass | 4 ◇ [2] | Pass |
| 5 ♣ | Pass | Pass | Double |
| All Pass | | | |

[1] Meaning, I believe, 'Have you anything better to suggest?' Perhaps this was the moment to bid three spades, the suit bid under him.

[2] Saying again, 'Pick a game'.

The play in five clubs doubled went like this: diamond ruffed, four of hearts won by South's king, five of clubs to West's jack. If Forrester had led the queen of spades at this stage he could actually have made the contract. South's ten of spades is pinned and declarer loses just a trump and a heart. Perhaps exhausted by the bidding, Forrester chose to run the nine of spades, eventually going two down.

At the other table, after the same start, Sowter raised to three diamonds over two diamonds. South attempted 3NT, which was doubled by East, and the final contract was four diamonds, one down. Britain won by 22–8.

*Sandra Landy, non-playing captain of the British Open team, holds the trophy for the winning team.*

# Britain v. France (ladies)

The French ladies have several very experienced players with international reputations, so in a way it was a little surprising that at the beginning of the 11th round they should lie sixth, three places behind Britain. They certainly looked very capable in this match. There were fireworks for the Open room audience as early as Board 2.

*North-South game; Dealer East.*

```
                    ♠42
                    ♡107
                    ◇AKJ6
                    ♣J9653
    ♠Q10987       ┌─────┐        ♠AJ65
    ♡J8           │  N  │        ♡K96432
    ◇5            │W   E│        ◇Q
    ♣Q10842       │  S  │        ♣AK
                  └─────┘
                    ♠K3
                    ♡AQ5
                    ◇10987432
                    ♣7
```

The French pair reached the obvious contract with this sequence:

| West | North | East | South |
|------|-------|------|-------|
| Guillaumin | McGowan | Cronier | Penfold |
| | | 1♡ | Pass |
| 1♠ | Pass | 3♠ | Pass |
| 4♠ | All Pass | | |

North began with the king of diamonds and South dropped the *ten*. What would you make of that?

In my old-fashioned way I would have thought it signified encouragement in diamonds, but apparently there were two other possibilities: it might have been thought to relate to the number of diamonds held and it might have been a suit-preference signal, asking for a switch to a high-valued suit.

North, at any rate, played a club at trick two. The declarer played another club, South ruffing. If South abandons hope of a trump trick now, she can simply exit with the king of spades and make two heart tricks later. Instead, she played a diamond, allowing a ruff-and-discard. West discarded a heart, ruffed in dummy, cashed the ace of spades and exited with the king of hearts. South had to win and a cross-ruff followed; excellent play by Guillaumin.

At the other table the contract was the same, but North led a heart at trick two, ensuring four tricks for the defence.

After being well behind at half time Britain recovered some points in the second half, for France to win 20–10.

*Elisabeth Hugon of France*
*contemplates the right lead.*

# Day Eleven

## Poland v. Ireland

If you pick up a continental magazine you will often find a story recording clever bidding or play by one of the numerous Polish players who seem able to participate regularly in pairs events all over Europe. This time they may have to tell a story against themselves.

*Love all; Dealer South.*

```
              ♠ 7
              ♡ A J 8 5 4
              ◇ 109632
              ♣ A 8
♠ K 109           ┌─────┐
♡ K 963           │  N  │
◇ 84              │W   E│
♣ K Q 10 5        │  S  │
                  └─────┘
```

South opened four spades and all passed. West led the king of clubs. The declarer, Balicki, won in dummy and played a spade to the queen and king. What now?

Pat Walshe made one of the best plays of the tournament — the king of hearts. See the effect of that:

```
              ♠ 7
              ♡ A J 8 5 4
              ◇ 109632
              ♣ A 8
♠ K 109           ┌─────┐      ♠ 64
♡ K 963           │  N  │      ♡ 7
◇ 84              │W   E│      ◇ A K Q 75
♣ K Q 10 5        │  S  │      ♣ J 9762
                  └─────┘
              ♠ A Q J 8 5 3 2
              ♡ Q 102
              ◇ J
              ♣ 43
```

When South took the king of hearts with the ace in dummy he was stymied with a stymie! There was no way in which he could regain the lead quickly. He tried a diamond, but East won and led a low club, to gain the heart ruff. That was lovely play.

## Ireland v. San Marino (ladies)

One of the pleasures of this championship has been the appearance of completely new teams such as Russia, Liechtenstein, Bulgaria, San Marino, and two 'infrequents', Czechoslovakia and Yugoslavia. Roumania and the San Marino Open team unfortunately had to withdraw at a late stage.

The San Marino ladies (San Marino, just in case you didn't know, is an enclave in northern Italy) have not greatly troubled the scorers, so I am happy to record a fine play made in their match against Ireland.

*Game all; Dealer South.*

```
              ♠ Q 8 5 3
              ♡ A 2
              ◇ A K J 8
              ♣ K 9 7
♠ 2                            ♠ 7 6
♡ Q 10 9 7 6 4      N          ♡ J 3
◇ 7 6           W       E      ◇ Q 9 5 3
♣ Q 6 5 3           S          ♣ A J 10 8 2
              ♠ A K J 10 9 4
              ♡ K 8 5
              ◇ 10 4 2
              ♣ 4
```

Playing in six spades, the declarer ruffed the third heart early on and reached this position, with the lead in her own hand:

```
              ♠ 5
              ♡ None
              ◇ A K J 8
              ♣ K 9 7
♠ None                         ♠ None
♡ Q 9           N              ♡ None
◇ 7 6       W       E   ·   ·  ◇ Q 9 5 3
♣ Q 6 5 3       S              ♣ A J 10 8
              ♠ J 10 9 4
              ♡ None
              ◇ 10 4 2
              ♣ 4
```

South led a club, West (enjoying her afternoon nap, I trust) played low, and the declarer put in dummy's nine.

# Day Twelve

## Britain v. Denmark

This was an important match for the British, who needed one more good result to make them strong favourites, while Denmark had been recovering from a moderate position. After a quiet opening the trend was set by:

*North-South game; Dealer East.*

```
                    ♠ None
                    ♡ A Q J
                    ◇ Q 10 9 7 4 3 2
                    ♣ Q 10 3
    ♠ Q                              ♠ 8 7 5 4 3 2
    ♡ K 9 8 7 6 5      N             ♡ 3
    ◇ J 6          W       E         ◇ A 8 5
    ♣ A J 7 5          S             ♣ K 9 8
                    ♠ A K J 10 9 6
                    ♡ 10 4 2
                    ◇ K
                    ♣ 6 4 2
```

This was the bidding in the closed room:

| West | North | East | South |
|------|-------|------|-------|
| *Sowter* | *Graulund* | *Smolski* | *Christiansen* |
| | | 2 ♡ | Pass |
| Pass | 3 ◇ | Pass | 3 ♠ |
| Pass | 4 ◇ | All Pass | |

East's two hearts was described as 'weak in spades or strong in hearts'. How anyone can develop an auction on that basis only heaven (and presumably Sowter) knows. However, it was easy on this occasion to conclude that East had the weak spade type. After a singleton heart lead against four diamonds the defence made two clubs, ace of diamonds, and a ruff, for 100 to East-West.

In the open room Adamsen opened an 8–11 one spade and the bidding continued:

| West | North | East | South |
|------|-------|------|-------|
| *Nicolaisen* | *Kirby* | *Adamsen* | *Armstrong* |
| | | 1 ♠ | Pass |
| 2 ♡ | 3 ◇ | Pass | 3 ♠ |
| Pass | 3 NT | Double | All Pass |

Since East-West were playing canapé style (shorter suit first) East's one spade might have been a three-card suit; so I suppose that South's three spades was natural. I still don't understand East's double.

East led a heart to the jack, captured the first diamond to shut out the dummy, and led a club to the ace. Then a club to the ten and king, and with the jack of diamonds falling, plus a defensive error later, North registered ten tricks for a swing of 1050 and 14 match points. That's how it goes when you are playing in good form.

*John Armstrong (right) discusses the Danish match with Tony Sowter and Roman Smolski.*

# Britain v. Denmark

Playing in good form (see previous page) is not always enough: you may have to play very well too. This was a later deal from the same match.

*North-South game; Dealer South.*

```
              ♠ 10 8
              ♡ K Q J 9 3
              ◇ J 10 5 4 3
              ♣ 9
♠ A K J 9                        ♠ Q 7 5 2
♡ 8 6 5 2      ┌─────────┐       ♡ 10 4
◇ 6 2         │   N     │        ◇ K 9 8
♣ 10 4 2     │ W   E   │        ♣ A 7 6 3
              │   S     │
              └─────────┘
              ♠ 6 4 3
              ♡ A 7
              ◇ A Q 7
              ♣ K Q J 8 5
```

The Danes played four hearts from the South side after a transfer. East-West cashed two spades and a club early on (moderate defence). With the diamond finesse right, there was no further problem. In the open room the hand was played by North after this sequence:

| West | North | East | South |
|------|-------|------|-------|
| *Nicolaisen* | *Kirby* | *Adamsen* | *Armstrong* |
|  |  |  | 1♣ |
| 1♡ | 2♡ | 3♣ | Double |
| 3♠ | Pass | Pass | 4♡ |
| All Pass |  |  |  |

A little mysterious, as usual. Apparently West's overcall of one heart signified length in both majors.

The defenders began with three rounds of spades, much more awkward for the declarer. North ruffed and led a club. Now East played a fourth spade. Declarer ruffed with the ace of hearts, leaving:

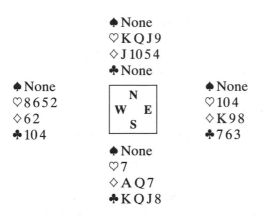

♠ None
♡ K Q J 9
◇ J 10 5 4
♣ None

♠ None
♡ 8 6 5 2
◇ 6 2
♣ 10 4

♠ None
♡ 10 4
◇ K 9 8
♣ 7 6 3

♠ None
♡ 7
◇ A Q 7
♣ K Q J 8

"He knows West has four hearts; he may play the odds and finesse the nine," boomed the chief commentator. But no! Kirby played king and queen of hearts. If the ten had not fallen he would have played a diamond to the queen and led winning clubs from the table, to West's misery. A great hand for the kibitzers. Britain finally won 25–5.

# Ireland v. Iceland

"People do like to read about the occasional mistake," Glyn Liggins, of BRIDGE magazine and Editor of this book, said to me. Then I don't see how I can possibly overlook this small affair!

*Game all; Dealer South.*

|  | ♠ K |  |
|---|---|---|
|  | ♡ 6 |  |
|  | ◇ J 10 9 8 4 3 2 |  |
|  | ♣ Q J 5 2 |  |
| ♠ 7 4 |  | ♠ Q J 10 8 6 5 |
| ♡ A K Q 5 4 3 | N | ♡ 10 9 8 |
| ◇ A K 6 5 | W   E | ◇ Q |
| ♣ 7 | S | ♣ A 10 9 |
|  | ♠ A 9 3 2 |  |
|  | ♡ J 7 2 |  |
|  | ◇ 7 |  |
|  | ♣ K 8 6 4 3 |  |

It's easy to go too high on the East-West cards. For example, if West bids an Acol-type two hearts and East responds two spades, following with strong support for hearts, West won't expect two spade losers. The counsel of perfection may be that when partner has opened a two-bid and you intend to support his suit you should avoid responding in any side suit that does not contain the ace or king; not that this would necessarily save you from calamity on the present deal.

The Irish North led his singleton trump against six hearts and Boland, South, did not cover dummy's eight. What do you suppose the declarer, Arnarson, did next?

He made a very smart play, I think, though it was lucky that the cards lay in a particular fashion. He led the ten of spades from dummy at trick two, just like a man who held the singleton king. Boland played the ace and his partner, Walshe, thought of revoking, but it wouldn't really have helped.

To cap the joke, the Irish at the other table bid to the same six heart contract, but the declarer did not find the same ingenious play at trick two.

*Terence Reese gathering the gen for this book.*

# Poland v. Netherlands

The bidding begins:

| West | North | East | South |
|------|-------|------|-------|
| 1 NT | Pass | 2♡ | ? |

South holds:

♠2　♡None　♢Q 10832　♣AKQ9632

It is love all and East's two hearts is the normal transfer (to spades). What should South say at this point?

Well, I doubt whether you will think of the clever move by Hans Vergoed, of the Netherlands. He passed. Why? Because it struck him that if he made any forward move the spade call might come from East, on his right; if he passed, then West would bid spades and he would be able to make a lead-directing double, perhaps at the six level. That's a tactical move I have not seen before. This was the deal:

*Love all; Dealer West.*

```
                  ♠8643
                  ♡87642
                  ♢J9
                  ♣87
   ♠Q107                        ♠AKJ95
   ♡AKQ105      ┌─────┐         ♡J93
   ♢A5          │  N  │         ♢K764
   ♣J104        │W   E│         ♣5
                │  S  │
                └─────┘
                  ♠2
                  ♡None
                  ♢Q10832
                  ♣AKQ9632
```

| West | North | East | South |
|------|-------|------|-------|
| 1 NT | Pass | 2♡ | Pass |
| 2♠ | Pass | 3♢ | 5♣ |
| Pass | Pass | 5 NT | Pass |
| 6♠ | Pass | Pass | Double |
| All Pass | | | |

The plan worked perfectly, to the extent that North led a heart and the slam was defeated.

You would expect a swing, would you not? But at the other table the sequence was:

| West | North | East | South |
|------|-------|------|-------|
| 1 NT | Pass | 2♡ | 5♣ |
| Pass | Pass | 5♢ | Pass |
| 6♠ | Pass | Pass | Double |
| All Pass | | | |

Again a heart was led, so the board was tied. Vergoed, it is said, was cross with East for bidding five diamonds (instead of five spades), but you can hardly blame the chap, can you?

## Germany v. Italy (ladies)

I asked Rixi Markus for her comments on this match, which she had watched the night before. "Sabine Zenkel's a very good player," she said. "One of the Italians was quite good, the other couldn't play at all, she must have been chosen because she is very pretty." The players concerned can take that either way.

Rixi's opinions about bidding were interesting, as always.

*East-West game; Dealer South.*

```
              ♠ Q J 6
              ♡ 4 3 2
              ♢ 9 5 4
              ♣ 8 6 5 2
♠ 9 2                        ♠ 7 5
♡ A Q J 9 8 5      N         ♡ K 10 7
♢ 7 3           W     E      ♢ K Q J 8 6 2
♣ J 10 3           S         ♣ A 9
              ♠ A K 10 8 4 3
              ♡ 6
              ♢ A 10
              ♣ K Q 7 4
```

It went one spade by the German South, pass, pass. 'Double?' I murmured, bidding for East. "That's terrible," Rixi declared. "There's only one call — three diamonds." Yes, this will probably be awkward for the opposition, and even when partner has a strong heart suit it is unlikely that you will be missing a game.

In practice the bidding continued:

| West | North | East | South |
|------|-------|------|-------|
|      |       |      | 1 ♠ |
| Pass | Pass | Double | Redouble |
| 3 ♡ | 3 ♠ | 4 ♡ | 4 ♠ |
| Pass | Pass | 5 ♡ | Double |
| All Pass | | | |

And East lost 500. Certainly her five hearts was wrong on a hand with so many losers, but four spades would presumably have been made, rather luckily.

Rixi made a good point about the play of the following hand:

```
♠KQ763          ┌─────────┐      ♠102
♡54             │    N    │      ♡AQ876
◇AQ106          │  W   E  │      ◇K95
♣A3             │    S    │      ♣K75
                └─────────┘
```

East plays in 3NT and South leads a low diamond. How should East set about the play?

Answer: play the diamond ten from dummy and, if it holds, lead a low spade towards the 10x. This much increases your chance of making spade winners.

## Standings after Round 24 (Day Twelve)

| | | | | |
|---|---|---|---|---|
| 1. | Great Britain | 487.5 | 14. Belgium | 349 |
| 2. | Sweden | 478 | 15. Finland | 345 |
| 3. | Poland | 442 | 16. Turkey | 338 |
| 3. | Iceland | 442 | 17. Ireland | 335.5 |
| 5. | Netherlands | 441 | 18. Austria | 334 |
| 6. | Italy | 419 | 19. Greece | 316 |
| 7. | France | 409 | 20. Portugal | 306 |
| 8. | USSR | 402 | 21. Bulgaria | 287 |
| 9. | Norway | 395 | 22. Switzerland | 283 |
| 10. | Israel | 392.5 | 23. Spain | 276 |
| 11. | Denmark | 387 | 24. Czechoslovakia | 275 |
| 12. | Germany | 374 | 25. Liechtenstein | 241.5 |
| 13. | Hungary | 362 | 26. Yugoslavia | 233 |

It looks close at the top, but Britain has the advantage. Britain has a bye, worth 18 points, and matches against Finland and Yugoslavia. Sweden has two byes and a match against Turkey.

The matches of the next three teams are going to create equal excitement, because four teams from this event will qualify for the world championship in Yokohama later in the year.

## Ladies Teams (16 Rounds)

With one round to go, the leading scores are Austria 331.5, Germany 314, Netherland 311. This means that Austria is virtually past the post. I will give the final scores when this round is over.

# Day Thirteen

## Denmark v. USSR (ladies)

There have been quite a few hands in the tournament where the declarer would have fared better if he had made a fairly normal hold-up with a holding such as Ax opposite xxx. It often makes a difference, in a way difficult to foresee, if you can deprive the opponents of the opportunity to go from hand to hand. There was an excellent example in this ladies match.

*Game all; Dealer North.*

```
              ♠ A Q 10
              ♡ 5 4 3
              ◇ J 7 4
              ♣ 10 9 7 6
  ♠ J 7 6                      ♠ 9 8 2
  ♡ A 8 2        N            ♡ K Q J 7
  ◇ Q 10 6    W     E         ◇ K 9 8 5 3
  ♣ Q J 5 4      S            ♣ 2
              ♠ K 5 4 3
              ♡ 10 9 6
              ◇ A 2
              ♣ A K 8 3
```

With Denmark North-South the bidding went:

| West | North | East | South |
|------|-------|------|-------|
|  | Pass | Pass | 1♣ |
| Pass | 1 NT [1] | Pass | 2♣ |
| Pass | Pass | Double | Pass |
| Pass [2] | Pass | | |

[1] In principle, 3–3–3–4 shape, so that if the opener has four clubs she can rebid the suit.

[2] With a partner who passed originally? The alternatives, two diamonds or two hearts or 2NT, are not attractive but are still much better than the pass.

West made a good lead, the ace of hearts, and the defence took three tricks in the suit. Then Easy led a low diamond and South won — a mistake, as we shall see. The declarer made ace of clubs, queen of spades, then played a second diamond. East won and now it was her turn: she should have led the thirteenth heart, ensuring two trump tricks for her partner, but instead she played a third diamond. Now it wasn't difficult for South to ruff, cash the winning spades and exit with a spade in this end position:

     ♣1097

♣QJ5       immaterial

     ♠5
     ♣K8

Poorish play by both East and South, but instructive. It was 180 against 90 for 1NT at the other table.

## Ladies Teams Final

| | | | | |
|---|---|---|---|---|
| 1. | Austria | 354.5 | 10. Sweden | 250 |
| 2. | Germany | 339 | 11. Ireland | 218 |
| 3. | Netherlands | 318 | 12. San Marino | 203 |
| 4. | Great Britain | 302.5 | 13. Spain | 200.5 |
| 5. | Denmark | 302 | 14. Turkey | 189 |
| 6. | France | 302 | 15. USSR | 180.5 |
| 7. | Italy | 282 | 16. Belgium | 178.5 |
| 8. | Israel | 271 | 17. Finland | 152.5 |
| 9. | Poland | 262 | | |

There is a big story about this. As the scores were originally announced, Britain were fifth. Three of the leading teams entered protests. Two were rejected, Britain's was partially accepted (see next page), and so Britain will qualify for the world championship in Yokohama.

Anyway, well done, Austria and Germany. The French, originally co-favourites, must be disappointed. Jean-Paul Meyer (editor of the main French magazine) tells me that their top pair, Willard and Bessis, played below their best form and that this seemed to affect the others.

Chris Dixon, the British captain, managed his team skilfully. They are not so far quite the class of the Americans, Canadians or Austrians, and the partners suffer from the disadvantage of living long distances (by British standards) from one another. But they improved a lot during the championship and may well make their mark in Yokohama.

# Britain v. Spain (ladies)

This was the dramatic deal that enabled Britain to finish
fourth and qualify for the world championship:

*North-South game; Dealer North.*

```
                  ♠3
                  ♡AQJ7654
                  ◇K108
                  ♣87
   ♠K10852                    ♠AQ9
   ♡108          N            ♡2
   ◇96         W   E          ◇Q752
   ♣10653        S            ♣AKQJ2
                  ♠J764
                  ♡K93
                  ◇AJ43
                  ♣94
```

| West | North | East | South |
|------|-------|------|-------|
| *Macaya* | *Smith* | *Duran* | *Davies* |
|  | 1♡ | Double | 1♠ [1] |
| Double [2] | 2♡ | 3♣ | 3♡ |
| 4♣ | 4♡ | All Pass | |

[1] The modern style when partner's opening bid has been
doubled is to make the same response (apart from pre-emptive
raises) as if there had been no intervention. Since I wouldn't
have responded one spade in any circumstances, I can scarcely
applaud it here.

[2] This was the call that led to the protest; not the call, exactly,
but the meaning attached to it. North was told by her screen-side
neighbour, East, that the double was responsive, indicating
general values.

The defenders cashed their black suit winners and then Nicola
played off all her trumps, reducing to three diamonds in North
and South. She played West for the queen and so finished
one down. The protest was based on the fact that on the
information she had been given, West should have held more
good cards than the king of spades, which was all she had
shown so far. At the other table East-West had played in
three clubs.

The Appeals Committee, with Solomonic wisdom, was unwilling to come down firmly on either side of the fence and awarded an 'in-between' score, crediting North with 'half a game'. The result of this — not known at the time, of course — was the British ladies, by the margin of half a point, qualified for Yokohama.

*Pat Davies watches nervously from dummy.*

# Netherlands v. Iceland

This was an important match between the teams lying fourth and fifth, out of touch with the leaders but competing for fourth (or third) place and the trip to Yokohama for the world championship. Iceland had much the better of the first half. Let me show what seems to me a good test of competitive judgement. South and West hold:

```
♠ A J 10 7 3          N
♡ Q 10 9        W          E
♢ Q 4 3              S
♣ A 8
                ♠ 8 4 2
                ♡ 4
                ♢ A 8 6
                ♣ K Q J 9 7 4
```

At game all the bidding goes:

| West | North | East | South |
|------|-------|------|-------|
| *Arnarson* | *Van den Brom* | *Jonsson* | *Mulder* |
|  |  | 2 ◇ | 3 ♣ |
| 3 ♡ | 3 NT | Pass | Pass |
| Double | All Pass |  |  |

East's two diamonds was the 'Multi', a weak two bid in one of the majors.

Two questions: was West right to double? Was South right to pass?

As for the first question, West had bid three hearts freely, so there was a good chance that his partner would lead a heart. Why give them a chance to escape from a bad contract?

As for the second question, of course he must run, with clubs headed by the K Q J only. The full hand was:

*Game all; Dealer East.*

```
                    ♠ K 6 5
                    ♡ A 6
                    ◇ K J 9 7 5
                    ♣ 5 3 2
    ♠ A J 10 7 3        N          ♠ Q 9
    ♡ Q 10 9      W         E      ♡ K J 8 7 5 3 2
    ◇ Q 4 3           S           ◇ 10 2
    ♣ A 8                          ♣ 10 6
                    ♠ 8 4 2
                    ♡ 4
                    ◇ A 8 6
                    ♣ K Q J 9 7 4
```

The Netherlands 3NT doubled went down 1100, a much better ending to the affair than West deserved. At the other table Iceland collected another 200 when four hearts by Leufkens–Westra went two off.

# Netherlands v. Iceland

The Icemen continued to hammer their Dutch opponents. Consider the play in five spades on this hand:

*East-West game; Dealer North.*

```
                    ♠ Q J 6 5
                    ♡ K 6 5 3
                    ◇ None
                    ♣ K J 10 6 3
     ♠ 10          ┌─────────┐        ♠ 2
     ♡ A 8 7       │    N    │        ♡ J 10 9
     ◇ A K Q 9 8 2 │  W   E  │        ◇ J 10 7 5 4
     ♣ 9 8 7       │    S    │        ♣ A Q 4 2
                    └─────────┘
                    ♠ A K 9 8 7 4 3
                    ♡ Q 4 2
                    ◇ 6 3
                    ♣ 5
```

| West | North | East | South |
|------|-------|------|-------|
| *Jonsson* | *Leufkens* | *Arnarson* | *Westra* |
| | Pass | Pass | 4 ♠ |
| Double | 5 ♠ | Double | All Pass |

West led the ace of diamonds, ruffed in dummy. South came to hand with a trump and led his singleton club. When West played low he put on the king. A heart return from East ran to the king. Nervous of running the jack of clubs after West's double, South tried vainly to ruff out the queen and had not enough entries to dummy to establish the fifth club.

The declarer had ten tricks from the beginning and probably his best play was a club from the table at trick two. Without taking any risks, he will succeed whenever the clubs are 4–3, and there are other possibilities.

At the other table North opened one diamond, described as Precision, though not my idea of the system. Baldursson played in four spades and make an overtrick.

From then on the Dutchmen faded badly, losing 25–2, a result that put Iceland in fourth place and destroyed the Netherlands hope of finishing near the top.

# Poland v. Switzerland

The penultimate day on Rama was highly entertaining, because the scores in four critical matches were shown. Poland and Iceland were competing for third place. This was Poland's last deal of the day:

*East-West game; Dealer West.*

```
              ♠ A 3
              ♡ A 9
              ◇ K J 8 4 2
              ♣ Q 9 7 5
  ♠ 7 5                         ♠ K Q 10 9 8 4
  ♡ Q 10 8 4 2    N            ♡ K 7 6 3
  ◇ 10 7 3     W     E         ◇ Q
  ♣ 1 0 8 6       S            ♣ A K
              ♠ J 6 2
              ♡ J 5
              ◇ A 9 6 5
              ♣ J 4 3 2
```

With Poland North-South the bidding went:

| West | North | East | South |
|------|-------|------|-------|
| Pass | Pass [1] | 2♡ [2] | Pass |
| 2♠ | Pass | 3♡ | Pass |
| 4♡ [3] | All Pass | | |

[1] The Polish strong pass.

[2] Most teams devised some counter to the strong pass. For the Swiss, bids at the one level were natural, but at the two level they amounted to a strong call in the suit above. There is some advantage in this, because the responder can bid simply two spades (as here) and the opener has room to pass or advance.

[3] A brave move on so little.

These contracts with three top losers and non-solid suits often fail, but on this occasion the Swiss were able to record 620.

Until this point it had looked as though Poland was going to take the bronze, but now, if Iceland could do the same as Switzerland and record 620 they would nose in front. Not quite; like most teams they had to report +170.

# Britain v. Spain (ladies)

The final round of the ladies event was extremely exciting. It was practically sure by this time that Austria, Germany, and the Netherlands would be the first three, in that order. Who would be fourth and qualify for Yokohama? Denmark, France and Britain were all in the fight. This was board 32:

*East-West game; Dealer West.*

```
                    ♠ 10 2
                    ♡ A K J 6
                    ◇ Q J 9 4 3
                    ♣ 4 3
    ♠ J 9 6 3              ┌─────────┐              ♠ 8
    ♡ 5 4                 │    N    │              ♡ Q 10 9 8 2
    ◇ 8 7 2               │ W     E │              ◇ K 5
    ♣ 10 8 7 6            │    S    │              ♣ A K Q J 9
                          └─────────┘
                    ♠ A K Q 7 5 4
                    ♡ 7 3
                    ◇ A 10 6
                    ♣ 5 2
```

Since four spades was bid and made at most tables, and the scores between the leading contenders were almost equal, the critical result was destined to be between Britain and Spain. The British pairs, Smith and Davies, bid the game with their usual competence:

| West | North | East | South |
|------|-------|------|-------|
| *Macaya* | *Smith* | *Duran* | *Davies* |
| Pass | 1 ◇ | 2 NT | 3 ♠ |
| Pass | 4 ♠ | All Pass | |

No problem here: South loses two clubs and a spade, recording 420.

At the other table:

| West | North | East | South |
|------|-------|------|-------|
| *Penfold* | *Kindeland* | *McGowan* | *del Villar* |
| Pass | Pass | 1 ♡ | 1 ♠ |
| Pass | 2 ◇ | 3 ♣ | 3 ◇ |
| Pass | 3 ♡ | Pass | 3 ♠ |
| Pass | 4 ◇ | Pass | 5 ◇ |
| All Pass | | | |

There were two poor calls in this auction: South's three diamonds (she should have bid three spades) and North's four diamonds (she should have bid four spades). Players seem not to realise that when you play in the lower of two possible suits you need to do *two* tricks better than the player in the higher suit. If you make eleven tricks and he makes ten you have gained nothing. South could not quite come to eleven tricks in diamonds. Britain had still just failed to qualify in fourth place, but the appeal described earlier put Britain in front of Denmark and France by the narrowest possible whisker.

*Liz McGowan of Britain.*

# Netherlands v. Liechtenstein

With one day to go, there was more excitement — at any rate, more uncertainty — at the bottom of the table than at the top. Yugoslavia and Liechtenstein had been contesting the wooden spoon for some while, and on round 26 Liechtenstein climbed ahead, thanks to the most critical deal of the day.

*Game all; Dealer South.*

```
                ♠4
                ♡AQ1096
                ◇K96
                ♣10652
  ♠732          ┌──────┐      ♠J9
  ♡KJ76         │   N  │      ♡84
  ◇10543        │ W   E│      ◇QJ82
  ♣J7           │   S  │      ♣KQ984
                └──────┘
                ♠AKQ10865
                ♡32
                ◇A7
                ♣A3
```

Six spades is a fair contract on the North-South hands. If a club is led, South will need the heart finesse and not too hostile a break in spades. Half the field finished in six spades, making, most of the others played in four spades or 3NT. Two pairs attempted seven spades; one failed, Carlo Palmieri of Liechtenstein succeeded.

After a trump lead the declarer took five rounds of spades, throwing a heart and three clubs from dummy. After queen of hearts, ace of hearts, heart ruff, the position was:

```
                ♠None
                ♡10
                ◇K96
                ♣10
  ♠None         ┌──────┐      ♠None
  ♡J            │   N  │      ♡None
  ◇1054         │ W   E│      ◇QJ2
  ♣J            │   S  │      ♣KQ
                └──────┘
                ♠6
                ♡None
                ◇A7
                ♣A3
```

Now ace of clubs, followed by the six of spades, drew the last breath from each opponent in turn.

The Dutch writer, Toine van Hoof, noted that the slam can be made even if West holds on to two clubs at the finish. The last eight cards will be:

$$\spadesuit \text{None}$$
$$\heartsuit \text{A Q 10 9}$$
$$\diamondsuit \text{K 9 6}$$
$$\clubsuit 10$$

```
        ♠ None              ┌─────────┐             ♠ None
        ♡ K J 7 6           │    N    │             ♡ 8 4
        ◇ 10 5              │ W     E │             ◇ Q J 2
        ♣ J 7               │    S    │             ♣ K Q 9
                            └─────────┘
```

$$\spadesuit \text{6 5}$$
$$\heartsuit \text{3 2}$$
$$\diamondsuit \text{A 7}$$
$$\clubsuit \text{A 3}$$

South cashes two diamonds, ending in hand, before playing the last two spades. West can throw a heart but then has to let go a club. Now the queen and ace of hearts (without benefit of the deep finesse) squeeze East in the minors.

# Day Fourteen

On the last day, with only one match to be played, there was nothing important to be settled except whether Poland or Iceland would be third. Poland just held on. With the journalists at their typewriters and the Bridgerama editors composing valedictory pieces, no outstanding hands were noted. Perhaps the most interesting feature of the day was that Yugoslavia, who had been bottom of the table since the first session, just managed to overtake gallant Liechtenstein. Final scores:

## The Open

| | | | | |
|---|---|---|---|---|
| 1. | **Great Britain** | 546.5 | 14. Turkey | 405 |
| 2. | **Sweden** | 527 | 15. Ireland | 392.5 |
| 3. | **Poland** | 504 | 16. Austria | 390 |
| 4. | **Iceland** | 503 | 17. Belgium | 388 |
| 5. | Italy | 479 | 18. Finland | 376 |
| 6. | Netherlands | 478 | 19. Greece | 360 |
| 7. | USSR | 463 | 20. Portugal | 348 |
| 8. | France | 455 | 21. Switzerland | 315 |
| 9. | Norway | 445 | 22. Bulgaria | 313 |
| 10. | Israel | 440.5 | 23. Czechoslovakia | 311 |
| 11. | Denmark | 437 | 24. Spain | 300 |
| 12. | Germany | 434 | 25. Yugoslavia | 258 |
| 13. | Hungary | 407 | 26. Liechtenstein | 256.5 |

## The Ladies

| | | | | |
|---|---|---|---|---|
| 1. | **Austria** | 354.5 | 10. Sweden | 250 |
| 2. | **Germany** | 339 | 11. Ireland | 218 |
| 3. | **Netherlands** | 318 | 12. San Marino | 203 |
| 4. | **Great Britain** | 302.5 | 13. Spain | 200.5 |
| 5. | Denmark | 302 | 14. Turkey | 189 |
| 6. | France | 302 | 15. USSR | 180.5 |
| 7. | Italy | 282 | 16. Belgium | 178.5 |
| 8. | Israel | 271 | 17. Finland | 152.5 |
| 9. | Poland | 262 | | |

# Final count

The event was a big success in every way, and a triumph for the British Open team, which evidently I underestimated in my earlier assessment. The great thing in the championships is not to have a bad spell, and this is where the team scored. Certainly they will challenge strongly in the world championships at Yokohama in September. There will be three American teams there, and the chances between them and the European leaders look very even.

One point that needs to be reviewed is the right action for the Tournament Directors and the Appeals Committee to take when different explanations of a particular call are given on the two sides of the screen. This is a problem that does not arise in what may be called the ordinary game. Personally I wish they would do without the silly screens for a year and see what difference it makes. In America they use screens only when they need to acclimatise their players to European practice. How did this screen business start, you may wonder. It was first tried in Sweden and then, in about 1971, it was supported by a V.I.P. in the bridge world and has remained ever since, despite the fact that a very high-class event like the *Sunday Times* Pairs goes perfectly without them. The essential thing is to teach players from the less 'professional' countries to bid with a good tempo.

A great many people contribute to the success of a tournament like this, some of them working for over a year. On my own behalf, in writing this book I have been helped especially by Bulletin co-editor Patrick Jourdain, commentator Barry Rigal, and 'kibitzers' Rixi Markus, Jean Besse, David Greenwood, and the two Danes, Ib Lundby and Peter Lund. My best thanks to all of them.

# Open Series

**AUSTRIA**
Franz Kriftner *(npc)*
Tilman Seidel
Andreas Babsch
Christian Terraneo
Alexander Wodniansky
Michael Barnay
Georg Kriftner

**BELGIUM**
Louis Saint-Georges *(npc)*
Michel Bolle
Guy Van Middelem
Olivier Neve
Claude Renard
Faramaz Bigdeli
Mike Zadika

**BULGARIA**
Mitko Mitev *(npc)*
Christo Droumev
Torkom Metchikian
Ivan Tanev
Ilko Bonev
Roumen Mantchev
Vladimir Filkov

**CZECHOSLOVAKIA**
Petr Jires *(npc)*
Ota Svoboda
Petr Hebak
Tomas Fort
Josef Kurka
Zdenek Illa
Zdenek Jelinek

**DENMARK**
Jens Kruuse *(npc)*
Villy Dam
Arne Mohr
Klaus Adamsen
Jan Nicolaisen
Soren Christiansen
Nis Graulund

**FINLAND**
Pekka Viitasalo *(npc)*
Kalervo Koistinen
Jouni Juuri-Oja
Kauko Koistinen
Mika Salomaa
Jorma Valta
Pekka Vihtila

**FRANCE**
Patrice Piganeau *(npc)*
Michel Abécassis
Philippe Cronier
François Leenhardt

Philippe Poizat
Jean-Christophe Quantin
Maurice Salama

**GERMANY**
Detlef Von Gynz *(npc)*
Jochen Bittschene
Georg Nippgen
Helmut Häusler
Bernhard Ludewig
Roland Rohowsky
Peter Splettstösser

**GREAT BRITAIN**
Mrs Sandra Landy *(npc)*
Tony Forrester
Graham Kirby
Tony Sowter
Andrew Robson
John Armstrong
Roman Smolski

**GREECE**
Dimitri Yallirakis *(npc)*
George Chnaris
Dionissisos Yannoutsos
George Karlaftis
Panayiotis Kannavos
Lucas Zotos
Alexander Lambrinos

**HUNGARY**
Jozef Pelikan *(npc)*
Miklós Dumbovich
Geza Homonnay
Mihály Kovács
Lazos Linczmayer
Gabor Macskássy
Lászlo Sziliágyi

**ICELAND**
Bjorn Eysteinsson *(npc)*
Jon Baidursson
Gudlaugur Johannsson
Gudmundur Arnarson
Adalsteinn Jorgensen
Orn Arnthorsson
Thorlakur Jonsson

**IRELAND**
Paddy Walsh *(npc)*
Nick Fitzgibbon
Paul Scannell
Pat Walshe
Adam Mesbur
Ray Brennan
Rory Boland

**ISRAEL**
Avri Peleg *(npc)*
Rami Porat
Nissan Rand
Yehuda Kaufman
Yoram Aviram
Shmuel Fridman
Gilad Altshuler

**ITALY**
Guido Resta *(npc)*
Lorenzo Lauria
Italo Santia
Norberto Bocchi
Fabio Rosati
Alfredo Versace
Giorgio Duboin

**LIECHTENSTEIN**
Alex Loesch
Vittorio di Silvio
Enzo dal Pozzo
Max Masla
Sergio Arnaboldi
Carlo A. Palmieri

**NETHERLANDS**
Enri Leufkens
Berry Westra
Leo v.d. Brom
Andre Mulder
Kees Tammens
Hans Vergoed

**NORWAY**
Runar Lillevik *(npc)*
Sam Hoeyland
Glen Groetheim
Sven-Olai Hoeyland
Geir Helgemo
Arne Thomassen
Helge Hantveit

**POLAND**
Mr. Lesniewski *(npc)*
Mr. Gawrys
Mr. Lasocki
Mr. Martens
Mr. Szymanowski
Mr. Balicki
M. Zmudzinski

**PORTUGAL**
Beatriz Debonnaire *(npc)*
Carlos Debonnaire
Rogerio Tadeu
Manuel C. Antunes
Acacio Figueiredo
Carlos Pimenta
Nuno Mascarennas

**SAN MARINO**
Filippo Fillippi *(c*
Giovanni Santag
Massimo Soroldo
Alberto Leornar
Andrea Fiaschi
Andrea Vignoli

**SPAIN**
Luis Lantaron
Ricardo Calvent
M. Angeles Mag
Federico Goded
Arturo Pardo
Jose F. Oliva

**SWEDEN**
Svante Ryman *(r*
Mats Nilsland
Anders Morath
Po Sundelin
Bjorn Fallenius
Sven-Ake Bjerre
Tommy Gullber

**SWITZERLAN**
Pierre Collaros *(*
Bui Minh Duc
Frédéric Dufaux
Hong Dong Duc
Tarek Yalcin
Allain Gaschen
Yvan Calame

**TURKEY**
Mr. Ozdil
Mr. Kubac
Mr. Dedehayir
Mr. Zorlu
Mr. Aydin
Mr. Assael

**USSR**
Vasily Levenko
Tim Zlotov
Sergej Baguzin
Tiit Laanemae
Michael Rosem
Andrej Spiridor

**YUGOSLAVIA**
Ranko Grba *(n*
Aleksander Bat
Radoje Antic
Momcilo Todos
Nenad Slipcevic
Momcilo Ignjat
Stevica Kikic

128

# Ladies Series

**AUSTRIA**
Ernst Pichler *(npc)*
Maria Erhart
Terry Weigkricht
Renata Fraser
Gabriele Bamberger
Doris Fischer
Helga Stiefsohn

**BELGIUM**
Louis Saint-Georges *(npc)*
Simone Azi
Lisette Berghs
Annie Loslever
Ghislaine Mortelmans
Caroline Vandenbossche
Sylvie Van Sichelen

**DENMARK**
Inge Keith Hansen *(npc)*
Tina Ege
Stense Farholt
Dorte Cilleborg
Trine Bilde
Judy Norris
Kirsten Steen-Møller

**FINLAND**
Ms. Siv Linden *(npc)*
Liisa Gronroos
Anja Hemila
Sari Kulmala
Mirja Mantyla
Eeva Parviainen
Barbro Vaaranen

**FRANCE**
Michel Bessis *(npc)*
Danielle Allouche-Gaviard
Véronique Bessis
Bénédicte Cronier
Catherine Guillaumin
Elisabeth Hugon
Sylvie Willard

**GERMANY**
Hans Gwinner *(npc)*
Daniela Von Arnim
Karin Caesar
Beate Nehmert
Sabine Zenkel
Marianne Mögel
Waltraud Vogt

**GREAT BRITAIN**
Mr. Chris Dixon *(npc)*
Elizabeth McGowan
Nicola Smith
Vi Mitchell
Sandra Penfold
Pat Davies
Jane Preddy

**IRELAND**
Kay Downes *(npc)*
Aileen O'Keeffe
Barbara Seligman
Evelyn Bourke
Rebecca O'Keeffe
Maria Barry
Diane Sloan

**ISRAEL**
Z. Ben Tovim *(npc)*
Migri Zur-Albu
Daniela Birman
Hanita Melech
Ruth Porat-Levit
Varda Abramov
Nurit Naveh

**ITALY**
Giovanni Maci *(npc)*
Monica Cuzzi
Carla Gianardi
Francesca de Lucchi
Marisa D'andrea
Gabriella Olivieri
Laura Rovera
(reserved pair:
G. Arrigoni/S. Falciai)

**NETHERLANDS**
Carla Arnolds
Bep Vriend
Ellen Bakker
Ine Gielkens
Marijke v.d. Pas
Elly Schippers

**POLAND**
Mrs. Mikucka
Mrs. Pasternak
Mrs. Raczynska
Mrs. Sendacka
Mrs. Harazimowicz
Mrs. Miedzychocka

**SAN MARINO**
Mimma Filippi *(cap)*
Nadia Stocovaz
Angela Rizzi
Barbara Pecchia
Carmen Capitini

**SPAIN**
Pilar G. Hontoria
Rosario Del Villar
Pilar Macaya
Pilar Leon
Beatriz Kindelan
Gloria Duran

**SWEDEN**
Kjell Swanström *(npc)*
Catharina Midskog
Lisbeth Astrom
Ylva Strandberg
Linda Langstrom
Marie Ryman
Lillemor Strindberg

**TURKEY**
Mrs. Goksu
Mrs. Kandiyoti
Mrs. Altinok
Mrs. Adut
Mrs. Taner
Mrs. Zorlu

**USSR**
Elena Borodic
Maja Romanovska
Olga Galaktionova
Svetlana Zenkevic
Natalia Karetnikova
Valentina Trusenkova

# RESULTS FROM THE OPEN IN KILLARNEY

| | BYE | AUS | BEL | BUL | CZE | DEN | FIN | FRA | GER | GBR | GRE | HUN | ICE | IRE | ISR | ITA | LCH | NTH | NOR | POL | POR | SPA | SWE | SWI | TUR | USR | YUG | TOTAL | RK |
|---|---|---|---|---|---|---|---|---|---|---|---|---|---|---|---|---|---|---|---|---|---|---|---|---|---|---|---|---|---|
| AUSTRIA | 36 | | 18 | 14 | 24 | 23 | 13 | 13 | 0 | 13 | 25 | 19 | 3 | 16 | 13 | 6 | 25 | 13 | 18 | 15 | 9 | 11 | 5 | 14 | 16 | 9 | 21 | 390 | 16 |
| BELGIUM | 36 | 12 | | 20 | 25 | 16 | 10 | 11 | 20 | 5 | 18 | 17 | 13 | 10 | 21 | 17 | 16 | 13 | 16 | 5 | 13 | 20 | 1 | 16 | 19 | 8 | 11 | 388 | 17 |
| BULGARIA | 36 | 16 | 10 | | 15 | 11 | 8 | 3 | 15 | 7 | 22 | 13 | 4 | 11 | 4 | 14 | 16 | 16 | 17 | 5 | 10 | 12 | 9 | 7 | 9 | 12 | 12 | 313 | 22 |
| CZECHOSLOV | 36 | 6 | 5 | 15 | | 7 | 12 | 18 | 9 | 4 | 8 | 12 | 13 | 18 | 11 | 19 | 25 | 3 | 13 | 11 | 22 | 16 | 6 | 25 | 6 | 0 | 3 | 311 | 23 |
| DENMARK | 36 | 7 | 14 | 19 | 23 | | 14 | 17 | 15 | 5 | 10 | 9 | 12 | 14 | 14 | 12 | 25 | 20 | 19 | 12 | 25 | 20 | 14 | 24 | 25 | 14 | 18 | 437 | 11 |
| FINLAND | 36 | 17 | 20 | 22 | 18 | 16 | | 8 | 11 | 9 | 5 | 5 | 3 | 24 | 13 | 8 | 19 | 12 | 10 | 15 | 19 | 14 | 11 | 22 | 1 | 7 | 25 | 376 | 18 |
| FRANCE | 36 | 17 | 19 | 25 | 22 | 13 | 22 | | 14 | 12 | 16 | 25 | 3 | 17 | 10 | 19 | 19 | 14 | 23 | 12 | 21 | 16 | 4 | 20 | 20 | 11 | 25 | 455 | 8 |
| GERMANY | 36 | 25 | 10 | 15 | 21 | 15 | 19 | 16 | | 9 | 15 | 18 | 9 | 17 | 17 | 11 | 21 | 5 | 12 | 13 | 17 | 25 | 9 | 25 | 21 | 15 | 20 | 434 | 12 |
| GR.BRITAIN | 36 | 17 | 25 | 23 | 25 | 25 | 21 | 18 | 21 | | 22 | 16 | 25 | 23 | 16 | 25 | 22 | 21 | 25 | 8 | 22 | 18 | 14 | 23 | 16 | 21 | 20 | 546.5 | 1 |
| GREECE | 36 | 5 | 12 | 8 | 22 | 20 | 25 | 14 | 15 | 8 | | 8 | 6 | 3 | 15 | 5 | 18 | 16 | 3 | 8 | 18 | 12 | 9 | 23 | 15 | 11 | 25 | 360 | 19 |
| HUNGARY | 36 | 11 | 13 | 17 | 18 | 21 | 25 | 4 | 12 | 14 | 22 | | 16 | 2 | 21 | 14 | 25 | 8 | 15 | 8 | 18 | 11 | 13 | 20 | 19 | 7 | 18 | 407 | 13 |
| ICELAND | 36 | 25 | 17 | 25 | 17 | 18 | 25 | 25 | 21 | 3 | 24 | 14 | | 21 | 9 | 15 | 25 | 25 | 9 | 8 | 23 | 225 | 16 | 25 | 21 | 15 | 23 | 501 | 4 |
| IRELAND | 36 | 14 | 20 | 19 | 12 | 16 | 6 | 13 | 13 | 7 | 25 | 25 | 9 | | 13 | 9 | 20 | 5 | 5 | 13 | 13 | 25 | 12 | 20 | 11 | 10 | 25 | 392.5 | 15 |
| ISRAEL | 36 | 17 | 9 | 25 | 19 | 16 | 17 | 20 | 13 | 14 | 15 | 9 | 21 | 17 | | 9 | 22 | 9 | 8 | 5 | 24 | 23 | 10 | 25 | 16 | 16 | 25 | 440.5 | 10 |
| ITALY | 36 | 24 | 13 | 16 | 11 | 18 | 22 | 11 | 19 | 5 | 25 | 16 | 15 | 21 | 21 | | 23 | 17 | 11 | 23 | 25 | 21 | 6 | 24 | 22 | 8 | 25 | 479 | 5 |
| LIECHTENST. | 36 | 3 | 14 | 14 | 3 | 4 | 5 | 11 | 9 | 8 | 12 | 0 | 1 | 10 | 8 | 7 | | 13 | 9 | 3 | 22 | 11 | 2 | 13 | 0 | 16 | 25 | 256.5 | 27 |
| NETHERLANDS | 36 | 17 | 17 | 14 | 25 | 10 | 18 | 16 | 25 | 9 | 14 | 22 | 2 | 25 | 21 | 12 | 17 | | 25 | 9 | 15 | 22 | 18 | 19 | 20 | 25 | 25 | 478 | 6 |
| NORWAY | 36 | 12 | 14 | 13 | 17 | 11 | 20 | 7 | 18 | 4 | 25 | 15 | 21 | 25 | 22 | 16 | 21 | 3 | | 9 | 25 | 25 | 15 | 16 | 13 | 14 | 25 | 445 | 9 |
| POLAND | 36 | 15 | 25 | 25 | 19 | 18 | 15 | 18 | 17 | 22 | 22 | 22 | 22 | 17 | 25 | 7 | 25 | 21 | 21 | | 13 | 17 | 9 | 18 | 17 | 15 | 23 | 504 | 3 |
| PORTUGAL | 36 | 21 | 17 | 20 | 8 | 3 | 11 | 9 | 13 | 8 | 12 | 12 | 7 | 17 | 6 | 4 | 8 | 15 | 4 | 17 | | 21 | 14 | 17 | 19 | 15 | 16 | 348 | 20 |
| SPAIN | 36 | 18 | 10 | 18 | 14 | 10 | 16 | 14 | 5 | 12 | 18 | 19 | 13 | 1 | 7 | 9 | 19 | 8 | 4 | 13 | 9 | | 12 | 1 | 5 | 0 | 11 | 300 | 24 |
| SWEDEN | 36 | 25 | 25 | 21 | 24 | 16 | 19 | 25 | 21 | 16 | 21 | 17 | 14 | 18 | 20 | 24 | 25 | 12 | 15 | 21 | 16 | 18 | | 17 | 13 | 23 | 25 | 527 | 2 |
| SWITZERLAND | 36 | 16 | 14 | 23 | 2 | 6 | 8 | 10 | 2 | 7 | 7 | 10 | 5 | 10 | 2 | 6 | 17 | 11 | 14 | 12 | 13 | 25 | 13 | | 22 | 8 | 18 | 315 | 21 |
| TURKEY | 36 | 14 | 11 | 21 | 24 | 3 | 25 | 10 | 9 | 14 | 15 | 11 | 9 | 19 | 14 | 8 | 25 | 10 | 17 | 14 | 11 | 25 | 17 | 8 | | 18 | 17 | 405 | 14 |
| USSR | 36 | 21 | 22 | 18 | 25 | 16 | 23 | 19 | 15 | 9 | 19 | 23 | 15 | 20 | 14 | 22 | 14 | 0 | 16 | 15 | 15 | 25 | 7 | 22 | 12 | | 23 | 463 | 7 |

# RESULTS FROM THE LADIES SERIES

| | BYE | AUS | BEL | DEN | FIN | FRA | GER | GBR | IRE | ISR | ITA | NTH | POL | SAN | SPA | SWE | TUR | USR | TOTAL | RK |
|---|---|---|---|---|---|---|---|---|---|---|---|---|---|---|---|---|---|---|---|---|
| AUSTRIA | 18 | | 25 | 22 | 25 | 25 | 14 | 8 | 24 | 23 | 21 | 23 | 13 | 25 | 20 | 22 | 22 | 25 | 354.5 | 1 |
| BELGIUM | 18 | 4 | | 11 | 18 | 4 | 0 | 2 | 17 | 4 | 0 | 6 | 18 | 8 | 8 | 18 | 22 | 21 | 178.5 | 16 |
| DENMARK | 18 | 8 | 19 | | 19 | 16 | 14 | 17 | 25 | 12 | 19 | 15 | 16 | 25 | 21 | 18 | 25 | 15 | 302 | 5 |
| FINLAND | 18 | 5 | 12 | 11 | | 4 | 1 | 5 | 5 | 7 | 9 | 15 | 11 | 8 | 12 | 5 | 8 | 17 | 152.5 | 17 |
| FRANCE | 18 | 0 | 25 | 14 | 25 | | 17 | 20 | 16 | 23 | 19 | 20 | 20 | 16 | 18 | 12 | 25 | 14 | 302 | 6 |
| GERMANY | 18 | 16 | 25 | 16 | 25 | 13 | | 14 | 23 | 17 | 25 | 19 | 14 | 23 | 25 | 12 | 25 | 17 | 339 | 2 |
| GR.BRITAIN | 18 | 22 | 25 | 13 | 25 | 10 | 16 | | 17 | 14 | 7 | 14 | 19 | 15 | 17 | 24 | 22 | 25 | 302.5 | 4 |
| IRELAND | 18 | 6 | 13 | 5 | 25 | 14 | 7 | 13 | | 13 | 6 | 0 | 20 | 4 | 25 | 11 | 14 | 24 | 218 | 11 |
| ISRAEL | 18 | 7 | 25 | 18 | 23 | 7 | 13 | 16 | 17 | | 8 | 4 | 9 | 25 | 25 | 10 | 21 | 25 | 271 | 8 |
| ITALY | 18 | 9 | 25 | 11 | 21 | 11 | 4 | 23 | 24 | 22 | | 4 | 11 | 16 | 21 | 13 | 25 | 25 | 282 | 7 |
| NETHERLANDS | 18 | 7 | 24 | 15 | 15 | 10 | 11 | 16 | 25 | 25 | 25 | | 12 | 25 | 25 | 23 | 9 | 23 | 318 | 3 |
| POLAND | 18 | 17 | 12 | 14 | 19 | 10 | 16 | 11 | 10 | 21 | 19 | 18 | | 10 | 21 | 25 | 6 | 15 | 262 | 9 |
| SAN MARINO | 18 | 3 | 22 | 1 | 22 | 14 | 7 | 15 | 25 | 3 | 14 | 1 | 20 | | 8 | 12 | 16 | 5 | 203 | 12 |
| SPAIN | 18 | 10 | 22 | 9 | 18 | 12 | 5 | 13 | 3 | 0 | 9 | 4 | 9 | 22 | | 17 | 9 | 20 | 200.5 | 13 |
| SWEDEN | 18 | 8 | 12 | 12 | 25 | 18 | 18 | 6 | 19 | 20 | 17 | 7 | 5 | 18 | 13 | | 22 | 25 | 250 | 10 |
| TURKEY | 18 | 8 | 8 | 5 | 22 | 1 | 3 | 8 | 16 | 9 | 5 | 11 | 24 | 14 | 21 | 8 | | 9 | 189 | 14 |
| USSR | 18 | 5 | 9 | 15 | 13 | 16 | 13 | 0 | 6 | 4 | 2 | 7 | 15 | 25 | 10 | 3 | 21 | | 180.5 | 15 |

# GENERALI TROPHY 1991

| RANKING COUNTRY | LADIES PAIRS | LADIES TEAMS | OPEN TEAMS | TOTAL |
|---|---|---|---|---|
| 1. GREAT BRITAIN | 16 + 2 | 84 | 160 | 262 |
| 2. NETHERLANDS | 13 + 12 | 96 | 80 | 201 |
| 3. SWEDEN | 14 | 12 | 144 | 170 |
| 4. Poland | 5 | 24 | 128 | 157 |
| 5. Italy | 9 | 48 | 96 | 153 |
| 6. Germany | 19 + 17 | 108 | - | 144 |
| 7/8 Austria | 18 + 1 | 120 | - | 139 |
| 7/8 France | 20 + 11 | 60 | 48 | 139 |
| 9. Iceland | - | - | 112 | 112 |
| 10. Denmark | - | 72 | - | 72 |
| 11. U.S.S.R | - | - | 64 | 64 |
| 12. Israel | 10 | 36 | 16 | 62 |

The European Bridge League congratulates the 1991 winners of the GENERALI TROPHY.